On the Plot

Also by Dirty Nails
HOW TO GROW YOUR OWN FOOD
A week-by-week guide to wild life friendly fruit and vegetable gardening

'This delightful book is a practical guide to enjoying the growing as much as the eating of your own food. It would be a stimulating book to encourage a beginner but being informative on many levels it is a really rewarding read for all who are willing to get their nails dirty.' *Reader review*

'What a wonderful book I have just read! It reads like a novel with the main character being 'Dirty Nails'. And what is it? A gardening book!! But it is more than that – wildlife, histories of various vegetables, soil information and for both the experienced and inexperienced gardener a week-by-week guide to planning, sowing, looking after and finally harvesting your very own veggies. Beautifully laid out and with a comprehensive contents page and extensive index, this is DEFINITELY one for the Gardener's library.' *Reader review*

'A delightful read. A "must" for ANY gardener. I felt so sad when I turned the page for the last week of January and found the year's week-by-week guide had finished. I wanted to just start all over again!' *Reader review*

'It is easy to imagine this book being consulted in garden sheds and allotment huts the length of the land, well thumbed in pursuit of another nugget of wisdom or vital piece of guidance from Dirty Nails. The sort of book any gardener would enjoy reading from cover to cover on a rainy afternoon.' *Fosse Way Magazine*

'A gardening book has got to be different, How to Grow Your Own Food is just that. This is a thoroughly enjoyable book which you could read at one sitting and delve into week by week.' *Mid Sussex Times*

'Packed with handy hints on wildlife-friendly fruit and veg gardening.' *Amateur Gardening*

'Thanks to his simple, down-to-earth style and chatty text,

Dirty Nails is well worth a read. A delightful walk through the veg garden year, this book will be invaluable to anyone who's still finding their feet amid the excitement of growing their own food.' *Garden News*

'A 208-pager filled with fascinating facts and useful jobs for each week of the year.' *North Devon Journal*

'A book, that down-to-earth gardeners will love. Anyone will learn a lot from his honest-to-goodness book.' *Organic Gardening*

'For any wannabe fruit and veg grower.' *Kitchen Garden*

'Every so often a book comes along that blows all that out of the water. This book is an absolute 'must have' for anyone serious about growing their own produce. Refreshing, easy to read in one sitting or to dip in and out of as a reference work, this book really does tick all the boxes. Plain common sense, humour and an amazing eye for detail.' *Grow It!*

'The detailed week by week commentary make it seem like the author "Dirty Nails" is standing right beside you giving you interesting and practical tips and advice throughout the year. It is an excellent inspiring book for both beginners and experienced gardeners alike.' *www.organic-gardening-tips.co.uk*

'A refreshing alternative to many of the glossy publications offered by garden centres and the like. A very tasty read!' *Dorset Wildlife Trust Magazine*

'This book does exactly what it claims to do. It has two pages for each week in the year all packed with information. The writing style is amusing from beginning to end and so easy to read. Over a year this book would give the amateur gardener a huge amount of information in an amusing and easily readable form. We thoroughly recommend it for gardeners and also as a birthday or Christmas present.' *Gardenaction*

Spring Hill is an imprint of How To Books Ltd.
Send for a free copy of the latest catalogue to:

howtobooks

Spring Hill House, Spring Hill Road
Begbroke, Oxford OX5 1RX, United Kingdom
info@howtobooks.co.uk
www.howtobooks.co.uk

On the Plot
with
'Dirty Nails'

A practical guide to fruit & vegetable gardening
– in words and pictures

Joe Hashman

'Dirty Nails' of the Blackmore Vale Magazine

SPRING HILL

Published by Spring Hill, an imprint of How To Books Ltd.
Spring Hill House, Spring Hill Road
Begbroke, Oxford OX5 1RX United Kingdom
Tel: (01865) 375794
Fax: (01865) 379162
info@howtobooks.co.uk
www.howtobooks.co.uk

British Library Cataloguing in Publication Data
A catalogue record of this book is available from the British Library

ISBN: 978 1 905862 32 0

Produced for How To Books by Deer Park Productions, Tavistock, Devon
Designed and typeset by Mousemat Design Ltd
Printed and bound by Ashford Colour Press, Gosport, Hants

NOTE: The material contained in this book is set out in good faith for general guidance and no liability can be accepted for loss or expense incurred as a result of relying in particular circumstances on statements made in the book. Laws and regulations are complex and liable to change, and readers should check the current position with relevant authorities before making personal arrangements.

Contents

Contents

Veg on the Menu: recipes

Acknowledgements

Cinzia Altobelli, for her fantastic, authentic Pomodori Con Il Riso dish featured in Veg on the Menu.

Seriously grateful thanks to Tony 'Bodger' Benge for understanding the vision and delivering in spades throughout a memorable year.

The Broadwindsor Allotmenteers (West Dorset) who made the scarecrow featured in October second week.

My neighbour John Cox, for sharing memories of a Warwickshire childhood and his mother's secrets from another time.

Many thanks also to my sister-in-law Deborah Ezekiel for her Spicy Sweet Potato Soup.

Sheila Gilbert, my stepmother-in-law, for various simple but effective recipes in Veg on the Menu, including Watercress Soup, Stuffed Cabbage and Stuffed Peppers.

Randy and Eugene Hiscock, for taking us out with their Suffolk Punches (August Week 2).

Everyone at How To Books, Deer Park Productions and Mousemat Design for keeping faith and investing time and effort in my ideas.

Nicola Keenleyside, for her badger photograph (August Week 5).

Victoria McManus, for her family heirloom Crapple Jelly recipe.

My step-daughter Hannah McQueen, for making a special Chocolate Strawberry Cake on my 40th birthday, and the Borsch.

Mrs Nails, as always, for putting up with my unsocial hours and all the trouble I cause!

Mum and Dad, for proof-reading and unconditional support.

Kate O'Farrell, for her wonderful whisky.

Finn Rawles-Malliagh, for helping with the onion harvest (September Week 4).

Robbie Redbreast, for posing so sweetly in November Week 4.

Frank and Faye Rutter, for supplying a dollop of handsome horse dung (August Week 2).

Pat Sennet, for her carpeted allotment (October Week 1).

Introduction

ABOUT THE AUTHOR

If you have ever dreamed about growing and cooking your own food, living the good life and getting close to nature then this is the book for you! Gardening and natural history enthusiast Joe Hashman serves up another absorbing helping of practical tips, advice and observations from his vegetable plot and kitchen.

Joe's popular weekly columns, written under the pen-name of 'Dirty Nails', have been enjoyed by readers of the Dorset-based Blackmore Vale Magazine since 2004. He now contributes to newspapers across England and Wales on a regular basis.

In this week-by-week account of the vegetable gardener's year, you are invited to join Joe on the plot and get stuck in to the important jobs of the day.

The finer points of crop husbandry are beautifully presented using clear and simple step-by-step photographs. With poetic licence in his writing, Joe takes the reader on a wonderful journey of discovery through the changing seasons. A wealth of easy to follow but unusual recipes will keep the chef in you busy and satisfied too!

Joe's first book, How to Grow Your Own Food, was published by How To Books in 2007 and received wide critical acclaim. His down-to-earth style and quirky tales from the garden continued with the release of A Vegetable Gardener's Year (2008). This latest volume stands alone as a manual for both the first time grower or seasoned expert, and also complements his earlier titles perfectly in the ongoing quest for survival on the plot.

TONY BENGE

Although no gardener, Tony's strong connection with the land and life that is dependent on it for food and habitat began as a five-year old when he moved from London to a remote Suffolk village. Crops were grown in every garden and on the three farms which for centuries had defined the village's way of living. Tony's weekly visits to Joe's plot during the year of photography which he has contributed to this book have refreshed many important memories and lessons about life's essentials, imprinted on his mind all those years ago.

February WEEK 1

Dunnocks

Spring is in the air. You can see it in the burgeoning green tips of daffodils, dangling hazel catkins releasing little yellow puffs of smoky pollen when rustled in the breeze or knocked by a passing gardener, sprouting seeds in pots and trays, lengthening days and changing light. The birds can feel it too. During a lull in the icy blasts of late-winter Easterlies they are thinking about breeding.

Dunnocks are the classic little brown jobs of birdwatchers' lingo but far more interesting than that description suggests. They are sparrow-sized with discreet brown bodies and grey heads. Their fluid, bubbling song is delivered in short musical bursts with no preamble and stops as suddenly as it starts. I've been watching a courting pair over the last few days. She sits on a branch, he alights close-by. They engage in mutual wing flickering as he sidles along towards her. Suddenly she is off and he is right behind. They play 'tag' amongst the tangle of branches, never far apart, as if joined by an invisible thread, communicating through delicate movement and dance.

Asparagus

The ideal time to plant asparagus crowns is March and April. To dovetail their arrival through the post with that period, ordering should be done now. I purchase mine from one of the many reputable dealers found in the classified section of specialist gardening magazines. There is a selection of varieties to choose from. Asparagus has only a short harvesting season in May and June. However, with careful attention paid to the cropping period of different strains, it is possible to extend the picking time slightly.

I suggest plumping for two-year old crowns of Connover's Colossal which, all being well, should yield stalks for cutting in two years' time. This is an early, thick-stalked asparagus which tastes fabulous. Crowns of this age will transplant readily if put into a properly prepared, well drained, sunny and sheltered bed immediately upon arrival. Bed-making, on previously enriched ground, is a job for the coming weeks.

The only consideration left at this stage is how many crowns to buy. They require plenty of room, 40cm between plants and 75cm between rows. Each fully mature crown will hopefully provide a couple of dozen stalks annually for the next fifteen or so years. All my family adore asparagus, so I've allowed for a considerable number of plants in my plans.

FEBRUARY WEEK 1

JOBS TO DO THIS WEEK

IN THE GREENHOUSE

- Check over all crops and newly-sown seed trays.
- Cover seed trays with fleece or newspaper at night if temperatures are really cold.
- Light a long-burning candle and place in a safe position under a clay pot at night to keep off frosty chill.
- Sow F1 Market Express turnip in trays.

ON THE PLOT

- Check over all areas.
- Adjust frost protection on globe artichoke crowns to keep them snug.
- Trim privet and other hedges.
- Split Marco garlic bulbs and plant each clove individually.
- Tidy Westland Winter kale by removing tattered, brown and yellowing outer leaves to the compost heap.
- Use a swan-necked hoe to draw soil up into ridges over dormant asparagus crowns on established beds.

Artichokes

Last autumn I potted on some globe artichoke chards (sprouting side-shoots). After being over-wintered in the greenhouse, they have thrown up handsome clutches of deeply serrated, silvery grey-green leaves. To make much-needed room for seed sowing, and to harden them off, the young plants were placed outside in a sheltered sunny spot this week. They will stay there until planting into their final positions during March. Each evening a double layer of fleece is secured over their tops as they acclimatise to life outdoors.

FEBRUARY Week 1: SOWING LEEK SEEDS

1. Fill a plastic tray with loam-based seed compost or multi-purpose alternative. Use a flat board to level and gently firm.

2. Sow the small black seeds thinly. Tap them out of the palm of one hand as evenly as possible.

3. Sprinkle a 3mm covering of compost through a sieve.

4. Dribble water to thoroughly moisten without soaking. Insert a label stating variety and date. Keep in the greenhouse or on a window sill.

February WEEK 2

Horseradish

This is a good week for cultivating horseradish. It is a vigorous, space-hungry vegetable that one nurtures in order to eat the thick, yellowish roots. Their pungent aroma and fiery taste makes for the perfect alternative to chilli at mealtimes, either grated on or into a dish.

When grown unhindered on the plot, horseradish is liable to develop an extremely deep and complicated root system. Pieces inevitably get left in the ground at lifting time. They re-grow readily, to the detriment of the next crop to occupy that space. Therefore, I'd advise raising horseradish in a 60cm deep bucket (minimum), filled with rich soil. Holes drilled in the bottom and a layer of small rocks and crocks will facilitate adequate drainage. The alternative is to devote a spare corner of the veg patch to this plant,

harvesting bits as and when required. However, it is apt to take over if not kept in check regularly.

Horseradish is easy to grow. Simply cut a 7.5cm piece of root with a sharp knife, square at the bottom end and slanted at the top. If leaf buds are present, reduce them to a single one. Pieces of root are then dropped into 12.5cm deep holes, standing upright and covered snugly with soil. With plenty of water and at least a little sunlight, large, coarse, deep-green leaves will be thrown up throughout the coming months, indicating plenty of activity underneath.

All being well, roots can be harvested the following October/November and stored in a frost-free box of moist sand. Another option is to keep oven-dried root shavings in airtight jars for use as a crispy, zingy garnish.

Crocuses

In the orchard, a scattering of last autumn's crocus plantings is peppering the dark earth with tufts of thin green-and-white striped leaves. They are a bit behind more established colonies elsewhere in the garden which have been displaying stunningly simple blooms of egg-yolk yellow and soft purple for some days now. But these new fellows take a little longer.

I was thrilled to spy the first one of many this week, slipping an elongated oval of delicate, fantastically-folded, dew-laden bud from its papery sheath. This streaky, pale, mauve-and-cream member is a tantalising taste of what will hopefully follow as dozens of these lovely spring flowers join forces with the fat bunches of peaking snowdrops and frilled yellow globules of aconite petals.

JOBS TO DO THIS WEEK

IN THE GREENHOUSE
- Uncover charges each morning if frost protection has been applied.
- Sow Roxton F1 leek, Tiger and Salad Bowl lettuces in trays.
- Sow Feltham First Early peas individually in pots.
- Remove pots where seeds sown in the preceding months have not germinated for washing, then store for further use.

ON THE PLOT
- Tidy old mushy leaves from cabbage patch. Remove them to the compost heap.
- Remove fleece protection from broad beans if weather is improving.
- Plant individual Aquadulce broad beans in the gaps where plants have succumbed to pests and harsh winter conditions. Pop them in 10cm deep at 15cm intervals.
- Plant bare rooted fruit trees when there is no frost in the ground.
- Admire the first crocuses of the season which may be flowering in the fruit garden.
- Plant pieces of horseradish root in a deep large pot.
- Weed out nettles and the first signs of germinating goosegrass (they are both edible so steam as greens or use in soups).
- Look out for frogs gathering to breed in the ponds.

Ravens

The distinctive cries of a passing posse of ravens the other morning caused me to stop what I was doing, straighten the old back and gaze towards the heavens. Three of these almost buzzard-sized, jet black members of the crow family were silhouetted high above. They flapped their long wings lazily, steering a course across a pale, early-spring sky that showed just enough blue to make a pair of sailor's trousers.

Ravens emit an easily identified, echoing call. It is deep and throaty, a honking croak quite unlike the friendly 'jacking' of jackdaws or altogether softer voice of carrion crows.

As a child growing up in the countryside five miles south of Oxford I never saw ravens. Now I'm always sure to make a mental note whenever these handsome birds chance to fly over. Having been banished from most localities by decades of misguided persecution their return as an integral thread in the fabric of the countryside marks an enlightening human approach towards sharing living space with other creatures.

FEBRUARY Week 2: PATHS

1. Paths should be constructed so as to allow comfortable wheelbarrow access. Narrow paths are awkward to manoeuvre and a source of frustration. Concrete paths offer a hardwearing, permanent fixture in the kitchen garden.

2. Grass paths are suitable for a rented plot such as an allotment. They are convenient and easy to establish. Grass demands regular mowing and edge-trimming during the growing season to keep neat and tidy and to prevent weeds setting seed.

3. A neat arrangement of bricks set into soil lends structure to a veg patch which is very pleasing. They instantly blend with an ageless look of natural permanence. Bricks can be left for years or shifted with minimal fuss as the garden evolves.

4. Wooden planks are perfect for affording temporary access across open ground. Instantly portable and made to measure, they protect the soil from becoming muddy and compacted.

February

Calendula

This week why not sow some calendula seeds? Also known as Pot or English Marigold and commonly reaching 45cm in height, this hardy annual sports prolific, handsome, daisy-like discs for flowers. Orange King and Art Shades are two varieties widely available, but now they're an established feature on the plot I simply use seed saved from last year. Collect it in paper bags on hot, dry afternoons during August. I am sure that you will be unfailingly rewarded with stunning, bold displays of vibrant oranges and yellows from May right through beyond October if the weather is kind.

Calendula is easily sown direct outside in a shallow drill where it is to flower, anytime from mid-March. But these are such simple, responsive and rewarding plants to grow that it is worth starting some off under cover now.

To this end, scatter some of the rough, knobbly, toenail sized-and-shaped seeds into a tray of moist compost and cover them to a depth of about 1cm. Kept moist (but not wet), they will be happy in the greenhouse or on a well lit windowsill.

When large enough to handle, or over-competing for space (depending on how thickly sown), prick some out into individual pots to cultivate indoors for a bit longer as specimens. The remainder will harden off for a few days, then go straight into the soil, their roots dangled down a finger-made hole and enveloped by the good earth gently pressed around them. They should romp away.

Bees love them, buds are edible in salads and petals provide an attractive garnish. At the end of the season, calendula provides good bulk for the compost heap.

Daisies

Spring comes and goes at this time of the year. Daisies on a sunny bank open widely to the warming afternoon sun in merry clumps, soaking up the energising rays. These pretty yellow-and-white, penny-sized flowers are the bane of many who seek to culture lawns purely of grass but to us wildlife-friendly gardeners they are a welcome, charming gift from nature.

Daisies are a constant theme throughout the years that keep on turning (it seems) with increasing speed from childhood. Old-timers say that spring has truly sprung when a maiden can place her foot upon seven in one go.

A mild spell early in the week had me believing we were nearly there. But only a couple of hours later, a flurry of dashing hail turned to the caressing hush of feather-soft snowflakes gently descending. A short time after, when clouds had passed, I retreated to a comfy chair indoors with freshly-laid fire blazing. The posy of daisies outside were with blooms shut tight awaiting more sunshine, hopefully in the morning.

FEBRUARY Week 3: BEAN TRENCHES & LETTUCES

1. In preparation for planting beans outside in May dig a trench in a sunny position, ideally running north to south for maximum exposure to sunlight. Excavate one spade-head (or 'spit') deep and long enough to service plants grown at 20cm intervals.

2. Discarded vegetable matter can be added bit by bit during the next few weeks. When the trench is full, cover over with soil and allow to settle. The refuse will decompose slowly and release nutrients into the 'root zone' which is exactly where they are needed the most.

3. Sow lettuce seeds into trays of multi-purpose compost on a window-sill or in the greenhouse now. Lettuce seeds are small and fiddly to handle. Use tweezers to sow them one at a time, 1cm deep. Keep them moist but not wet.

4. As soon as the seedlings are large enough to handle, prick them out into individual 9cm pots of John Innes Number 1 compost.

FEBRUARY WEEK 3
JOBS TO DO THIS WEEK

IN THE GREENHOUSE

- Keep a tender daily eye on what is going on in the protected greenhouse environment.
- Apply dribbles of water where needed, but be careful not to soak compost too much.
- Keep a candle burning under a clay pot at night to keep the temperature just above freezing.

ON THE PLOT

- Check over all standing crops and areas of bare earth.
- Trim leylandii hedges.
- Use fleece or straw to protect globe artichokes and other standing crops such as celeriac from really cold night temperatures.
- Dig trenches in preparation for planting First Early potatoes next month. Enrich with compost or well-rotted manure.
- Clean and trim plot edges. Carefully tease out couch grass ('twitch') and bag this up for burning, not composting.
- Mark out rows for Second Early, Maincrop and Salad potatoes with canes and string. This really helps to orientate what is going where on the plot.
- Harvest the last of the Dwarf Green Curled kale. Remove plants and bash tough, woody stems with a hammer before chucking on the compost heap. Alternatively, if the ground space is not urgently need, allow spent plants to stand and flower later. Early insects find the simple blooms of brassicas extremely useful and attractive.

Ramsons

In the lanes hereabouts, from mossy, ivy-clad, hazel-topped banks, shiny green leaves of ramsons (wild garlic) are unfurling from the edges like hares' ears. They provide a strongly flavoured treat for the walker who munches on a few tender, gathered pieces, adopting an aroma that will linger all day.

Mrs Nails, however, prefers to use them sparingly in a late-winter salad. This comprises portions of thinly sliced leeks and carrot strips, the freshest, youngest, budding tips of curly kale and ramsons' leaves (both shredded), a drizzle of olive oil, balsamic vinegar and a squeeze of lemon juice.

February

WEEK 4

Preparing Peas

The initial under-cover sowings of Feltham First Early peas, made at the end of January, are growing strongly. They are stout and healthy, up to 5cm tall, with two tendrilled leaf branchlets and a leading shoot ready to go. With white roots visible from the bottom of the pots, these peas have grown well and will soon be ready for planting outside.

In preparation for this I have been hardening off my dozen-and-a-half tiptop looking specimens this week. Hardening off only entails putting the peas outside each morning where they can bask in any available sunshine and placing them back in the greenhouse come evening time.

I also think it's a sensible thing to feed and warm the ground where they are to reside. To this end, dig a trench one spit (a spade head) deep, fill it with well rotted manure (peas like plenty of goodness) and cover it back over with soil. A cloche pegged down over the bed and kept in place throughout the coming days should raise the temperature slightly. The idea is to make a comfortable home for this sweet-tasting crop in the near future.

Rummaging Robins

Every now and then a bird turns up in the garden looking a little the worse for wear. Most years there will be one or two blackbirds who have survived a cat attack. It may be that these are resident blackbirds anyway and once scalped their bald appearance makes them readily identifiable. Mrs Nails always christens such birds 'Columbo', after the dishevelled, shuffling TV cop. We take great pleasure from watching their antics. They become friends who excite much celebration when they appear each day.

This week, whilst having a break from digging three long rows of First Early potato trenches, I was entertained by a chirpy robin. Red-breast descended on the freshly disturbed earth to gobble up as many soft-bodied soil creatures as possible. 'Robbie' (the name I use when referring to all visiting robins) had also been in a scrape. Through binoculars, it was clear that the whole right side of the little chap's face was recovering from some sort of damaging injury. How it was caused was unclear. Whether a pleasure-seeking cat, or sparrowhawk trying to survive the winter was responsible is open to conjecture. Robins are also fierce fighters at this time of year and such damage could even have been inflicted during a territorial tussle with another male.

Thankfully Robbie seemed okay and was bobbing and hopping from clod to clod with one bright eye shining, judging intricate take-offs and landings perfectly, and having a jolly good rummage in search of a meal.

FEBRUARY WEEK 4
JOBS TO DO THIS WEEK

IN THE GREENHOUSE

- Ventilate in the mornings.
- Daily, remove Feltham First Early peas to the outdoors during daytime to harden off and bring them back into the greenhouse at night.
- Sow Pentland Brig and Habholer Grun Krausner kale in pots.
- Sow Swiss chard.
- Cover tender seedlings and chitting spuds with fleece at night if temperatures threaten to dip very low. Cover a lighted candle with clay pot to keep frost at bay.
- Sow Mange Tout and Sugar Snap peas.
- Sow Musselburgh leeks and Lobjoits Green Cos lettuces in trays.
- Sow Egor and Wellington F1 Brussels sprouts in pots.

ON THE PLOT

- Keep digging trenches for planting potatoes.
- Empty contents of compost heap into trenches.
- Harvest Brussels sprout tops for 'spring greens' then remove plants to the compost heap. Beat stems to a pulp before leaving them to rot.
- Remove frost protection from globe artichokes if weather permits.
- Prepare ground for early direct sowing of peas: dig a trench, fill with well-rotted manure, cover over with soil and put a cloche over the top to warm the ground slightly.
- Check over fruit trees.
- Top dress established asparagus bed with sprinkling of sea salt and organic fertiliser.

Stroking Seedlings

Stroking your seedlings might seem slightly weird, but many including myself consider it to be an essential job where plants are raised in a protected environment. With no wind or air currents to gently rock and buffet emerging shoots and leaves, growth is liable on occasion to be rather weak and spindly. Therefore, spending time each day in the greenhouse simply stroking each of your emergent and juvenile charges with the back of your finger is time well spent! It aids their development by stimulating good rooting and structural strength from an early age.

Aubergine and tomato seedlings are on a sunny windowsill in the warmth of the house. Their position by the telephone ensures that each of these very well looked-after plants is jogged and tickled a few times each day.

FEBRUARY Week 4: TOOLS

1. FORKS: *Potato*, with many tines close together to cradle and lift spuds when digging, even the tiniest tuber. *Garden*, for cultivating soil, spearing and moving composts and manures. *Border*, small and light, ideal for tickling between rows of veggies. *Kitchen*, for delicate close-up weeding.

2. HAND-TOOLS: *Secateurs* for pruning. *Trowels* for planting, weeding or making drills. *Dibber*, for planting leeks, also sometimes spuds and cabbages. *Bent knife*, perfect for weeding in tight spaces. *Hand fork*, preferred by some over using a trowel when working on hands and knees.

3. SPADES: *Border*, light and easy on the back. Good when working close to standing crops or in flower beds. *Digging*, for inverting clods of soil and excavating holes. *Shovel*, the best for lifting and shifting soil, compost, leafmould and gravel amongst other things.

4. HOES: *Draw*, or 'swan-necked', for earthing up spuds, making wide flat-bottomed drills for crops like peas, and leveling out uneven ground. *Dutch*, or 'push', is the number one tool in the battle with weeds. *Watering can*, use the largest you can comfortably carry to keep plants moist but not wet.

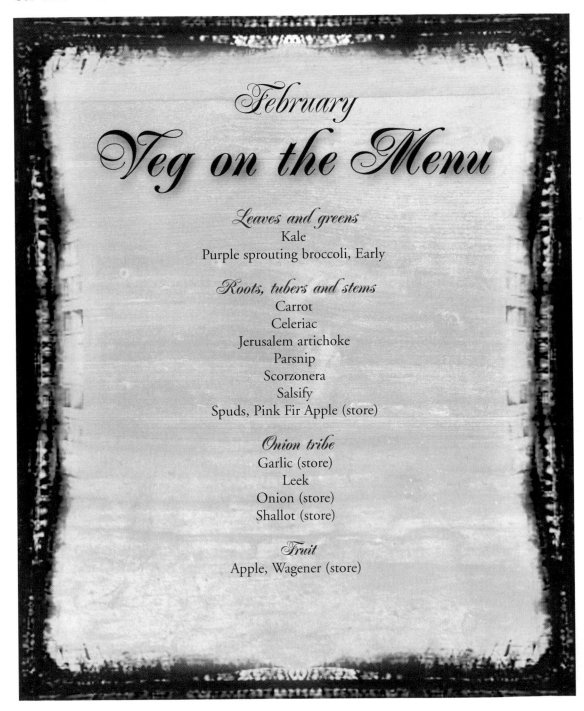

February
Veg on the Menu

Leaves and greens
Kale
Purple sprouting broccoli, Early

Roots, tubers and stems
Carrot
Celeriac
Jerusalem artichoke
Parsnip
Scorzonera
Salsify
Spuds, Pink Fir Apple (store)

Onion tribe
Garlic (store)
Leek
Onion (store)
Shallot (store)

Fruit
Apple, Wagener (store)

March WEEK 1

Preparing and Planting Asparagus

Hours slogging away during the winter months, readying a plot of land for an asparagus bed, is time productively spent. And now spring is well and truly here. Just step outside and feel the rushing, pulsating surge of life all around.

This week is an ideal time for final preparations in expectation of that box of Special Delivery two year old crowns arriving at the front door in the postman's arms any day soon. Asparagus crowns appreciate being planted on the day of receipt, or as soon as possible afterwards, so digging their trenches in advance ensures a swift bedding-in.

A well-prepared bed could crop for 15 or 20 years if consistently looked after and nurtured, so every careful consideration must be given to the location. A sunny and sheltered aspect with well-drained soil is ideal. The selected plot should be enriched with as much available organic matter as the home-producer is able to muster over the previous few months.

Asparagus crowns need plenty of room. 40cm between the spread-out roots in rows 75cm apart is perfect. I mark the rows out with canes and string to keep them straight, then dig a trench to the depth of one spit (a spade head) and 30cm wide, to accommodate the roots when splayed. Removed soil is deposited to the side of the trench, ready to backfill later. Wherever land is sloping I put dug soil on the top side. This makes dragging it back to refill less of an effort.

Once unpacked on the day of arrival, I think it's a really good idea to totally submerge the fragile crowns in a bucket of water for an hour prior to getting them in the ground. This soaking will rejuvenate them after their travels and allows you time to fine-tune those prepared trenches, tailoring them precisely to meet the requirements of your new residents. To this end, work along each trench with a spade to make a fairly 'clean' excavation. Loose soil and debris that has fallen in is fashioned so as to create a shallow ridge along the middle of the trench bottom.

The crowns, which resemble small-bodied spiders or many-fingered hands, are brittle and dry out easily. The roots demand teasing apart carefully. Having done this, sit the crowns atop the shallow ridge with their roots spread in all directions down the sides. Cover each one immediately with 12.5 cm of earth before repeating the task with the next until, one by one, the job is done. Keep them in the bucket of water right up until the point of planting.

Nothing should be cut in the first year after planting. A little soil can be drawn around the green shoots with a swan-necked hoe as they appear. They must be allowed to grow freely and then re-absorb all the goodness at the end of summer to build up strength. A small portion of spears may be harvested the following year and the remaining soil drawn over the rows. Full-blown production (and eating!) occurs subsequently - from the third year after planting.

However, there is always much to do. The lover of this delectable crop will work hard to keep his or her asparagus bed well watered and weed free throughout the summer. No deep rooters (such as dandelion or dock) are permissible because once the crowns are in position any further digging will only damage their roots.

MARCH Week 1: SOWING BROAD BEANS

1. Mark out rows with canes and string over weed-free soil raked level. If sowing a double row, allow 20cm between parallel lines.

2. Large seeds feel substantial in the hand. Select the biggest and most handsome.

3. Plunge seeds 5cm deep at 12cm intervals. Work from wooden boards to prevent delicate soil from becoming compacted.

4. Protect newly-sown seed from birds, with wire or string. Support netting with jar-topped sticks or canes.

MARCH WEEK 1

JOBS TO DO THIS WEEK

IN THE GREENHOUSE
- Ventilate in the mornings.
- Pot on Dynamite lettuce seedlings.
- Water trays and pots if needed.

ON THE PLOT
- Cover and uncover globe artichokes day and night if frost threatens.
- Check over all areas and think about what will go where.
- Enjoy the heart-lifting sight of crocuses amongst the fruit trees and other beautiful early spring sights.
- Liquid feed winter purslane.
- Plant out Feltham First Early peas into prepared ground.
- If mild, plant out Vanessa and Winston varieties of First Early potatoes.
- Sow Witkiem broad beans.

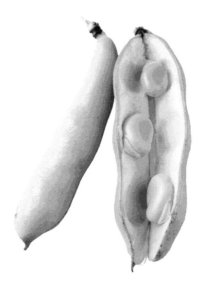

March

Badgers

This week I've been thinking about badgers. I know that there are some who really don't like these fascinating beasts but they're a permanent fixture in my neighbourhood. I consider that they are the original residents here. Their subterranean labyrinthine setts and tunnels honeycomb the green sandstone underlying fertile loams and clays in which I cultivate my crops.

I respect the fact that Brock was dug in to the landscape well before roads and houses sprung up all around. The amazing fact that the badgers are not just hanging on but thriving is a testament to their amazing tolerance and adaptability. It feels like an honour to have three sett complexes within spitting distance of the veg plot. The scrabble-scratch of their claws on paths as they turn tail and scamper away when disturbed after dark, or a thrilling glimpse of their powerful, stocky, low-slung frame and wonderfully striped head in the half-light of dusk or on moonlit nights never loses its magic for me.

However, there is no disputing the fact that these black and white fellows can do damage in a well-tended garden. Mrs Nails has given up growing tulips in certain places because the bulbs of this lovely flower are like tasty chocolate bars to badgers. The lawn, too, takes a beating as they scrape and snuffle in search of worms and grubs. On occasion,

the compost bucket will be turned out in the yard if Young Master Nails chucks in a half-eaten pizza last thing at night. But who can blame the badger, for he is only doing the same as we all are, trying to make a living.

'Billy' loves root veg, which includes carrots, parsnips and potatoes. I suffer heartbreak just like anyone else when carefully-tended crops are occasionally trashed. Precautions can be taken, however, and I am pleased to successfully grow carrots (a badger favourite) year after year. The trick, and I learnt this from the Old Timers locally, is to douse the area daily in the growing season with human urine dispensed from a spray bottle. A friend grows her carrots in earth-filled drums out of harm's reach and also reports complete satisfaction.

March is a busy time of year for badgers. Cubs were born last month and family life for these communal creatures is in full swing. The other day, a neighbour politely asked if I could stop 'my' badgers from getting into his garden and rooting around in the borders. My reply was slightly tongue in cheek when I said that I'd have a quiet word and ask them to avoid that garden as they do their nightly rounds. The reality is completely different, of course. These are wild animals who freely come and go as they have done for generations, treading the same well-worn paths as their ancestors before them. A little smelly stuff sprayed here and there is only a short-term deterrent.

The gardener who is frustrated by visiting badgers needs to consider either (1) erecting fencing buried deep into the soil to prevent them getting over or under, (2) appreciating them for the beautiful, intelligent animals that they are, tolerating and learning to love their boisterous behaviour whilst adopting gardening regimes to minimise conflict, or (3) moving to another area completely.

Meanwhile, in the orchard (a quiet corner set aside for wildlife), I continue to put out biscuits, nuts, and scraps for local badgers each night. Brock (their old English name) is especially fond of licking off honey or sugar and salt-free peanut butter smeared onto a rough log. What's the difference between doing this and feeding the birds? In my opinion, putting out rations for wildlife provides an intimate relationship with the wider world which transcends the day-to-day trials and tribulations of modern living.

MARCH Week 2: SOWING PARSNIPS

1. Sow parsnips between mid-February and May. Grow them in light soil which has not been recently manured and is ideally stone free. This encourages the roots to plunge deep in search of moisture and nutrients.

2. In cold weather parsnips can be sown indoors into cardboard tubes filled with multi-purpose compost. Use tweezers to handle. Sow three per tube and thin to the strongest seedling. Then plant tubes whole outside at 15cm intervals.

3. Outdoor sowings should be made into 2cm-deep drills which were moistened in advance. Do it on a calm day or the confetti-like seeds will blow away. They are slow germinators so be patient! Two months later they might look like this.

4. Parsnips taste best after the first autumnal frosts have made them sweet. They will be happy in the ground as a 'standing crop' all winter until needed in the kitchen.

JOBS TO DO THIS WEEK

IN THE GREENHOUSE
- Ventilate in the mornings.
- Tend to watering of seedlings daily.
- Harden off Dynamite lettuce by putting outside in the day and bringing back into the greenhouse at night.
- Seed sowing might be in full swing by now but don't worry if the trials of life prevent you from getting on with it - there is still ample time and slightly later sowings will soon catch up in the warmer weather to come.

ON THE PLOT
- Prepare a bed for onions: weed meticulously, sprinkle wood ash, rake level, do the gardener's shuffle.
- Clear spent kale plants to the compost heap.
- Tidy plot edges by removing wiry threads of encroaching couch grass and turning spoil inwards to create a shallow ditch between path and productive soil.
- Employ the hoe in dry sunny spells to annihilate weeds.
- Have a good sorting and tidying session in the shed in preparation for the coming season.

MARCH

WEEK 3

Butterflies & Other Insects

Whilst sitting on the bench treating my face to a drench of warm spring sunshine, and as an excited Mrs Nails got down to some serious flower seed sowing in the greenhouse at the start of this week (sweet peas, love-in-a-mist, cosmos, clary sage), I was treated to the pretty vision of my first butterfly on the wing this year. The pale yellow insect fluttered by, skimming the carpet of splayed, basking crocuses, now flowering in the orchard. It was a brimstone. The subtle plain yellow colouration of this lovely creature, slightly paler on females, is what puts the word 'butter' into butterfly. Brimstones hibernate over the winter under loose tree bark and amongst thick ivy. Invigorating rays of sunshine will raise them from their slumbers (even as early as February if the weather is mild), urging them to venture forth from such hidey holes. Primroses are a favourite flower of theirs. The relationship is mutually beneficial: the brimstone receives sustenance and the flower is pollinated in return.

In the warm early spring sunshine I watched, fascinated, as a queen wasp clambered up and out from the sawdust, debris and twigs on the floor of the wood-store. She spent many minutes preening and stretching before climbing to the summit of a length of wood and falling off again.

In her semi-torpid state, the wasp appeared as much mechanical as animal, her legs working slowly and deliberately as she steadied herself. Undeterred, queen dragged her strikingly bold segmented yellow-and-black striped body to the bottom of a wooden post and determinedly commenced a long haul to the top.

By now, the sun had shifted position in the sky and the woodpile was in shade. The wasp rested three-quarters of the way up. At this point, I felt compelled to assist (or 'interfere', as Mrs Nails would say!). Using a small stick I deposited a drop of honey (normally reserved for the badgers) next to the exhausted queen, hoping that it would boost her strength.

Upon my return from chores elsewhere, the queen was nowhere to be seen. If she establishes a nest somewhere safe in the vicinity of the garden (a hedge would be ideal, but preferably not in the shed) where the wasps can prey on caterpillars and grubs throughout the summer, thus keeping cabbages and Brussels sprouts clean and strong, I shall be happy to share my space with these much maligned insects.

Fruit Tree Maintenance

Developing a strong and healthy root structure in the formative years is important for ensuring long-term health and productivity in 'top fruit' (apples, pears, plums, cherries and the like). Be mindful to pour at least two large cans full of water around the base of each of tree if rain holds off for long enough for the soil to dry. Thoroughly good soakings throughout the first few growing seasons will pay dividends in years to come.

Lettuces

Dynamite lettuce seedlings, sown undercover towards the latter half of January, have been potted on this week. The rate of lettuce growth in optimum conditions is amazing and the Dynamite variety is no exception. Within a matter of only days delicate tufts of tender young leaves barely 2.5cm or so across will double in size and an early harvest of crunchily refreshing-yet-mellow sandwich filling or baked potato accompaniment is in the offing.

When they are showing at least two leaves (apart from the initial seed leaves) tap the tiny plants out of their 7.5 cm pots, keeping the root ball as intact and undisturbed as possible. Hold them tenderly by the leaves and support the roots with a small flat stick (a lolly stick is ideal). Transfer your young charges into larger receptacles with a little fresh potting compost at the bottom, firmed gently round the edges and moistened. 10cm pots are ideal. Then give your lettuces pride of place in the greenhouse. They can go outside in a sunny, sheltered position soon.

MARCH Week 3: GARDEN WILDLIFE

1. The crocus provides bumblebees with an extremely important source of sugary nectar early in the season when there is little else about. It gives them energy and strength. Plant some around fruit trees or wherever you imagine ground will remain relatively undisturbed.

2. Lay off the pesticides to attract natural predators like ladybirds. Females deposit about 200 eggs which hatch into miniature monsters like the one pictured. In the three weeks it takes before changing into an adult each individual will eat hundreds of aphids.

3. Prehistoric frogs are welcome on the plot because they eat loads of pests including slugs. Create a wildlife pond without goldfish - they eat the tadpoles. Leave uncut areas and piles of logs where frogs can hide safe from cats.

4. Grow the Butterfly Bush *Buddleia davidii* around your plot edges to attract beautiful butterflies and other useful insects. Small tortoiseshell butterflies, like the one above, often hibernate through winter amongst thick evergreen ivy, so leave that growing up big trees as well.

MARCH WEEK 3
JOBS TO DO THIS WEEK

IN THE GREENHOUSE

- Check over and tend seedlings.
- Water daily.
- Ventilate in warm weather.
- Pot on lettuces.
- Harden off Dynamite lettuces and peas.
- Sow Premier cabbage, Rhubarb Leaf Swiss chard, Giant Single sunflower.
- Physically stroke seedlings to strengthen stems and stimulate roots.

ON THE PLOT

- Water potatoes, greens and winter onions well if springtime is dry.
- Apply a bucket of water each to all young and newly planted fruit trees.
- Keep the hoe busy.
- Do a spot of hand weeding whenever you have a moment to spare.
- Water broad beans and rhubarb.
- Plant out Stuttgarter Giant and Turbo onion sets into prepared ground.
- Deliver sacks of horse manure to the plot. If it is fresh, put away somewhere to quietly rot down for future use.
- Erect netting for newly-sown peas to scramble up in due course.
- Plant out second sowing of Feltham First Early peas.
- Plant out F1 Market Express turnips sown in early February.
- Sow another short line of F1 Market Express turnips to crop in succession.
- Sow Boltardy beetroot and French Breakfast radish.
- Plant out Dynamite lettuces sown in January.
- Plant out peas which have been hardened off.
- Remove frost protection from globe artichokes and tidy the crowns.
- Plant out Red Baron onion sets.
- Pull any remaining brassica plants and bash up the woody stems before consigning to the compost heap.

March

Celeriac

This is a good week for sowing celeriac seeds. These handsome vegetables are also known as 'turnip-rooted celery' on account of the bulbous, swollen, edible stem that sits on the soil surface. A mat of fine roots explore the ground underneath, fan-like, searching out moisture and nutrients.

Celeriac thrives on a rich site and responds well to regular soakings throughout the growing season, especially if rainfall is in short supply. Alabaster is widely available, easy to grow and a good cropper of knobbly, pock-marked portions. Prinz and Mars are two varieties which are smoother. Why not enjoy cultivating a selection of all three? A sowing made now will, all being well, be harvestable from October when fist-sized.

Start your plants off by sowing the minute, ridged, oval seeds in trays in the greenhouse. With the aid of tweezers, pop them in at 5cm spacings to a depth of no more than 1cm or so and cover lightly. Watering the trays must be done delicately and with care, so as not to disturb the tiny seeds unduly. Then place a pane of glass on top and shade this with newspaper. Remove it when the first seedlings begin to appear, hopefully in about three weeks time.

When approximately 5cm in height, and large enough to handle, prick out the seedlings and grow them on in individual pots before planting out in their final resting places towards the end of May or in early June. At that stage, be sure to nestle them in very shallow at 30cm intervals in rows 45cm apart. Subsequently, celeriac only demands to be kept moist and weed free.

Celeriac will sit quite happily fresh in the ground over most of the winter to be harvested as and when required. In really harsh conditions it can be protected with a covering of straw or bracken. Flavoursome celeriac is distinctive and delicious, boiled in a mash or eaten raw, cut into strips for dips or grated. Mrs Nails adds aromatic leaves to winter soups and stews for an excellent celery substitute.

Bud-Burst

One of the great things about gardening, as far as I'm concerned, is that it provides for us all an ongoing and intimate relationship with the natural world and the magical associated seasonal rhythms and cycles. Who can fail to be continually amazed and impressed by the way things just seem to happen when nature is left to her own devices? For example, and there is nothing unusual or rare about this scene, beyond the back wall boundary a carpet of ferny-leaved cow parsley greenery jostles for light and space with thick, deep-green and chocolate-spotted wild arum leaves. The latter unfurl and force their way vertically out of the earth then assume a more horizontal position, like great lush arrow-shaped spatulas clumped around the woodland floor.

A cold and unusually dry late winter/early spring this year has delayed the greening up of deciduous trees and bushes, but with substantial rain arriving in the last few days (of the soft, gentle, persistent variety as opposed to short, sharp, destructive deluges), buds are bursting all around. These weeks when the leaves are all coming out in various stages arguably provide one of the most exciting spectacles that the year has to offer.

In my sheltered plot a fan-trained Morello cherry is always first or thereabouts in the bud-burst department. Over the preceding few days, tiny shiny brown pimples have swollen and enlarged. Now, the tip of each wondrously enclosed package is breached and interlocking scales are parting. The leaves, resembling miniature toggles, tightly folded and pale-green, are barely recognisable in this state. I'm keeping my fingers crossed that each bud will also be full of blossom.

Subsequent fine helpings of dark cherries (I hope) are perfect for high summer culinary delights or, if left on the tree a little longer, a few heavenly mouthfuls as nature intended. The birds will be after them too, so precautions will need to be taken to keep them off.

Late frosts can be damaging to trees which blossom early. Crops can be ruined. To prevent this keep a fleece handy. Be ready to drape it over blooming trees should the forecast deem this wise. It is an easy job to do, especially when a tree is grown flat against a shed or wall.

MARCH Week 4: RADISHES

1. Radish seeds are large enough to handle individually. Sow in 2cm-deep drills at 2cm spacings. Cover with soil, firm gently, keep moist and weed free. Sowing like this reduces the need for wasteful thinning out later.

2. The French Breakfast variety can be succession-sown at fortnightly intervals all summer long for continuous supplies of chunky, crunchy, peppery roots. Pull when their bright red shoulders stand proud of the soil.

3. Munchen Bier radishes produce flowers and spicy seed pods with which to garnish salads. The delicious roots can attain tennis ball-sized proportions and are cooked like turnips.

4. Neckarrum is an icicle-shaped radish which can be eaten large or small and always tastes hot. Perfect for sowing late July/August for autumn consumption.

MARCH WEEK 4
JOBS TO DO THIS WEEK

IN THE GREENHOUSE
- Sow a tray of Carentan leeks.
- Sow Prinz and Mars celeriac.
- Pot on all tomatoes, including Early Pak 7, Tumbler, Red Alert and Ailsa Craig.
- Pot on tomatillo Verde.
- Pot on D'Orlando corn salad.
- Ventilate in the mornings.
- Attend to watering daily.
- Sow American land cress.
- Pot on Salad Bowl lettuces.
- Commence nightly torch-light slug patrols.

ON THE PLOT
- Mourn the loss of F1 Market Express plants to the munching attention of either slugs or snails!
- Keep collecting manure and leaves wherever you find these valuable soil-improving materials. Store in old compost bags.
- Apply well-rotted manure to potato trenches.
- Hoe and hand weed amongst winter onions.
- Plant Second Early (Kestrel) and Maincrop (Picasso and Nadine) potatoes.
- Fork over thoroughly-weeded bed earmarked for parsnips and rake to a fine tilth ready to sow seeds.
- Sow Adelaide F1 carrot, North Holland Blood Red and Ishikura spring onions.
- Erect pea netting for recent plantings of this fabulously delicious crop.
- Set beer traps amongst Dynamite lettuces to thwart slugs and snails.
- Hand weed amongst winter purslane.
- Sow Hablange White and Tender & True parsnips.
- Sow Long Black scorzonera, Sandwich Island salsify and Zefa Fino Florence fennel.
- Have a cup of tea early each morning and listen to the birds.

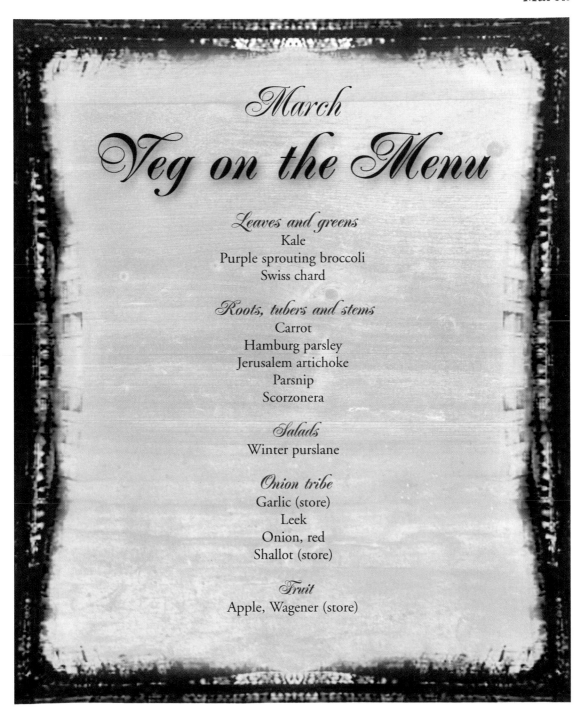

March
Veg on the Menu

Leaves and greens
Kale
Purple sprouting broccoli
Swiss chard

Roots, tubers and stems
Carrot
Hamburg parsley
Jerusalem artichoke
Parsnip
Scorzonera

Salads
Winter purslane

Onion tribe
Garlic (store)
Leek
Onion, red
Shallot (store)

Fruit
Apple, Wagener (store)

April

Florence Fennel

This week I have been sowing seeds of Florence fennel. My variety of choice is Zefa Fino, which will hopefully provide thick, flat bulbs as big as the palm of my hand throughout the high-summer months. Steamed, roasted, or eaten raw, the distinctive aniseed-like flavour of this vegetable is a welcome addition on the dinner plate. Pinches of the delicate but strong-tasting ferny foliage can also be taken throughout the growing period to freshen up salads.

Florence fennel performs best in rich, well-drained soil that is kept moist. Plenty of sunshine is needed too. I prepare my fennel bed by raking the previously dug growing medium into a fine tilth and removing any seeds that are trying to gain a toe-hold.

I'd suggest choosing a warm dry day in April to mark out rows 30cm apart with canes and string. Employ your finger or the tip of a trowel to carve out a shallow drill 1.5cm deep, using the string as an aid to straightness. Moistening the drill before sowing is a good idea to jolly along germination. Dribble water along its furrowed length at this point in the proceedings and then sow the pinhead-sized seeds directly afterwards. Take care at this stage to distribute the seed thinly but evenly along the drill. Then brush soil back over to cover. In order to nestle them snugly into their new home, gently 'tamp' the good earth down with the back of a rake.

This unusual looking vegetable can grow surprisingly large with the addition of its stalks radiating like a green peacock's tail-fan, so I think aiming to cultivate Florence fennel at intervals of 30cm is wise. Be quite brutal over the next few weeks at thinning out weaker seedlings and young plants in order to afford your chosen specimens access to the space and goodness they need for big bulb production. A consistent supply of water to avoid prolonged dry spells, regular hoeing in the vicinity and hand weeding closer in, combined with a decent summer weather-wise (which we all enjoy!) should do the trick.

Chiff-Chaffs

Right on cue, with the arrival of April came the returning chiff-chaffs. It is very pleasing when the delicate patter of these 11cm long, pale grey-yellow birds is once again part of the garden soundscape. I'm fond of these diminutive warblers, not least because their call is distinctive and fairly easy to recognise. It instils confidence in those of us who want to make sense of the sights and sounds of our little patches.

The soft but far-carrying single-noted song is lovely, floating as it does over the veg plot in harmony with a sunny blue sky. It can be interpreted as the bird's name - 'chiff-chaff, chiff-chaff' or 'chiff-chiff-chiff', a dozen or more times, pause, and repeat.

Delivery is from high up in trees and bushes. They have a habit of singing a bit, then dropping down low before fluttering and zig-zagging to the top again for another round. At other times, these feathered songsters are more difficult to see than hear, hopping and flitting deep within the tangled thickets where they prefer to nest.

APRIL Week 1: SOWING GLOBE ARTICHOKES

1. Globe artichokes form bushy clumps of coarse, silvery-grey leaves and are at home in flower borders or a regimented vegetable patch. Seeds are large enough to handle individually. Simply nestle them into small pots of compost about 1.5 cm deep and keep moist but not wet.

2. Seed leaves, or cotyledons, erupt from the surface in a matter of days (as shown). Nurture seedling artichokes in their pots until around midsummer. They thrive with space, moisture and sunshine so plant into rich soil allowing a clear metre all round.

3. Exquisite-tasting edible buds are produced in the second and subsequent seasons from June until October. Here is the main, or 'king' bud, in a basket of summer veg. Cut buds with about 5cm of stem attached. Boil until tender.

4. As members of the thistle family, globe artichokes provide nectar and shelter for insects and food for seed eating birds in winter. Spent flower heads can also assume an architectural beauty during the long cold months if left standing on the plot.

APRIL WEEK 1

JOBS TO DO THIS WEEK

IN THE GREENHOUSE

- Check over all crops.
- Sow different varieties of kale: Dwarf Green Curled, Pentland Brig, Habholer Grun Krausner, Thousandhead, Nero di Toscana.
- Sow Premier cabbage and Patrick F1 kohl rabi.
- Patrol greenhouse nightly with a torch to seek and evict slugs and snails.
- Pot on Swiss chard seedlings.
- Sow tomatillo Verde.
- In pots, sow French Breakfast radishes, Amsterdam Forcing carrots and White Globe turnips.
- Keep all seedlings moist but not wet.
- Harden off plants on the verge of being planted out.
- Sow various lettuces, including Buttercrunch, Dynamite, Little Gem, Tiger, Lobjoits Green Cos, Great Lakes.
- Sow Greenshaft and Mange Tout peas in deep pots or toilet roll tubes.
- Sow Pure Gold and Kelvedon Glory sweetcorn.
- Prick out pot marigold (Calendula) seedlings.

ON THE PLOT

- Potter productively: whenever you visit the plot do something useful on the way even if it is only just fetching and carrying.
- Plant out potted-up globe artichokes that have been carefully nurtured through the winter. Give them plenty of room to grow big.
- Get busy with the hoe whenever the sun is shining.
- Keep winter onions weed free.
- Tidy and mulch around step-over apple trees.
- Dig a trench for planting runner beans in May. Fill it with well-rotted manure, cover over and allow to settle. Mark the position with canes and string.
- Keep container-grown strawberries well watered.
- Plant out lettuces, corn salad and summer cabbages in a sunny bed with protection.
- Hand weed here and there while weeds are still small, especially goosegrass and willowherb. The former makes great eating when stir-fried or steamed like spinach!
- Check recently planted maincrop onions daily until their roots have anchored into the soil. Replace any turfed out by the weather, birds or cats.
- Plant container-grown fruit trees. Bardsey Island/Afal Enlli apple is an unusual and remarkably disease-free eater that is well worth a try.
- Hoe amongst the garlic and shallots.
- Harden off lettuces and peas on the cusp of being planted outside.

April

WEEK 2

Stinging Nettles

Stinging nettle tips are an important part of the dinner-time menu at this time of year which is traditionally known as the 'hungry gap'. Most over-wintering veggies in the kitchen garden have now been harvested and the present season's flush of edible goodies are yet to fill the plate. This is when the humble and ubiquitous stinger comes into its own.

There are always plenty growing around the edges of the plot. A carrier bag can easily be filled with their tender tips. Early in the season nettles have yet to become loaded with their potent defensive poison so foraging gardeners are able to pinch out the topmost four leaves without even wearing gloves. They are actually quite delicious and full of goodness when cooked in the same way as spinach or other greens. There are few easier crops to grow.

Mrs Nails likes me to mix a collection of nettles, curly kale, sprigs of purple sprouting and steam them all together at once.

APRIL Week 2: LEEKS & LETTUCES

1. Prepare a nursery bed for leeks. Rake to a fine tilth, moisten with water. Then, with a cane or stick, make 5cm-deep holes at about 8cm intervals in a grid.

2. Tease seedling leeks from their trays carefully. Place one per hole with roots nestled in. Trim these slightly if necessary. Don't close the hole, just water with a rose on the can. Soil falls naturally over the roots. Keep moist and weed free until after mid-summer.

3. Lettuce seedlings can be planted outside now. Harden off for a few days then lift from trays with a forked spatula ('widger') keeping roots and compost as intact as possible. Handle with care from leaf only, never the stem.

4. Allowing 20cm between individuals, open a pocket in weed-free soil with fingers or a trowel. Lower roots into this, fold back round and firm. Water occasionally if the weather is dry. Pick individual leaves when big enough or harvest whole heads in a few weeks time.

APRIL WEEK 2
JOBS TO DO THIS WEEK

IN THE GREENHOUSE

- Check all crops with regard to their health and watering needs.
- Conduct nightly slug and snail patrols with a torch. Any time betwixt 10pm and midnight should be well worth the effort.
- Ventilate well.
- Sow Rocula Coltivata rocket, Rhodynda Red and January King cabbages.
- Sow Early and Late purple sprouting broccoli.
- Set up a box of compost and mushroom spores to see if you can get a decent crop (follow the instructions provided).
- Young kale and Brussels sprout plants can start to be hardened off, but do remember to bring them in at night.
- Amongst the whoosh of April growth don't panic! Take your time and enjoy precious moments in the greenhouse tending your charges.
- Sow Tagetes marigold, dill and chamomile in trays.
- Sow Minipop F1 sweetcorn, Marketmore and Bush Champ cucumber, Hispi F1 cabbage.
- Sow squashes: Marina di Chioggia, Vegetable Spaghetti, Uchiki Kuri, Butternut Waltham.
- Sow Bianca di Trieste, Soliel F1 and Nero di Milano courgettes.

Sparrowhawk

The swift and deadly predatory skills of a sparrowhawk were in evidence one afternoon this week when a couple of mates and I were quietly sitting in the garden having a blokey natter.

Out of the blue, a flash and crash in the greenhouse and in the blink of an eye, exiting through the open door, a powerfully flying specimen of this dashing bird of prey. Long brown-and-cream barred wing undersides and the shattered rag of a small bird held in tightly gripping claws dangling underneath told the story: one had inadvertently become disorientated after flying into the greenhouse, the other had spotted an easy target and executed the dramatic mealtime raid at break-neck speed.

We could scarcely believe our eyes and were somewhat taken aback. Later, examination of puffs and tufts of soft feathers on the greenhouse floor gave few clues as to the victim's identity, save for confirming that the amazing 'Nature, red in tooth and claw' event really had occurred.

APRIL WEEK 2
JOBS TO DO THIS WEEK

ON THE PLOT

- Keep a fatherly or motherly eye on your plot and what is going on.
- Hand weed here and there.
- Secure fleece around Brown Turkey fig being grown as a fan against a south-west facing shed. Keep it in place for the time being.
- Thin out radishes sown towards the end of March.
- Trim plot edges with long-handled edging irons. Evenings are a good time to do this as this job is very relaxing and mellow.
- Trim burgeoning vegetation around soft fruit bushes.
- Hand weed around newly planted and established globe artichokes.
- Pop down to the woods and collect some hazel pea sticks for future use.
- Sow Tardel beetroot and Amsterdam Forcing carrots.
- Plant out Lobjoits Green Cos lettuces.
- Apply an obstructive barrier around lettuces to keep slugs and snails off.
- Set up hazel pea sticks for supporting Mange Tout peas.
- Mow grass paths.
- Plant out pot marigold seedlings in lines around the edges of the plot.
- Hand weed the asparagus bed.
- Harden off brassicas.
- Plant out Swiss chard.
- Employ the hoe for some gentle weeding.

April

WEEK **3**

In The Greenhouse . . . Turnips

The greenhouse is full and bursting with emergent life at the moment. Every available piece of shelf is hosting an array of veg and flower seedlings in pots and trays. It's a hive of activity, although before I had the luxury of growing veg in a protected environment, window sills and sunny spots in the house were utilised instead.

It has been possible to steal a march on the long cold spring this year by starting more crops than usual indoors. Lettuces and turnips, for example, have shown little movement as direct outdoor sowings, with slugs and snails accounting for the entire length of a two-metre line of F1 Market Express 'nips as soon as they began to show. So I've resorted to cultivating these earthy-tasting roots in pots with 5 to 7.5cm spacings, in much the same way as one might grow early cropping radishes.

. . . Lettuces

Lettuces are easy to bring on in the greenhouse at this time of year, before excessive summer heat inhibits germination. I recommend getting a selection of Little Gem Pearl, Buttercrunch, Great Lakes, Lobjoits Green Cos, Dynamite and Tiger varieties on the go. If you sow them in small trays of shallow compost at the start of April and keep moist but not wet, they should be mostly all up now and doing well.

Be mindful of future summer salads and sandwiches: get this medley of lettuces outside when they are large enough to handle, beginning to jostle for space, and strong enough to withstand the loss of a leaf or two to munching molluscs.

. . . Squash

Mid-April is the ideal time for planting squash seeds. You can do just that this week. There are many different varieties to choose from, each with its own individual eating and keeping qualities.

A particular favourite in our house is the unusual Spaghetti Squash. This is a reliable cropper of rugby-ball sized fruits when blessed with plenty of water and sunshine. Pop the flat, fingernail sized seeds, one per 7.5cm pot and 2.5cm deep into moist compost. Ensure that they are inserted into the growing medium on their edges to minimise any risk of the seeds rotting if they are kept too wet.

Given a well lit position in which to bask, germination should occur in a few days. Spaghetti Squashes need to be kept under cover until all risk of frost has passed (around mid-May, a couple of weeks later in the North) and then planted outside into compost-enriched holes with 60cm of growing room all around. Heavy, oval, pale-skinned squashes develop on the ground along the sprawling branches of this plant. They ripen as summer passes.

Mrs Nails is rather partial to roasting Spaghetti Squash in large chunks, whereupon the flesh can be pared off the skin with a fork. It has a wonderfully rich and delicious flavour, coming away in a multitude of spaghetti-like shreds (hence the name), providing substantial and interesting portions to accompany an autumnal roast dinner.

. . . Celeriac

Sown towards the end of March, celeriac seedlings should now be starting to emerge. Immediately upon sowing, I recommended covering the trays with glass and newspaper. With a few delicate Prinz seedlings now up, remove the shade and protection. All being well, within a couple or three days the majority of Prinz and Mars will be showing tiny pairs of oval leaves on white stalks. Allow them to grow considerably larger and sturdier before pricking them out into pots prior to planting outside.

APRIL Week 3: HOEING

1. Aim to pass the blade back and forth through the top layer of soil with small, smooth strokes, slicing the weeds off from their roots. Straddle seedling rows and work backwards.

2. The hoe is number one tool in the battle with weeds. Employ a small file to keep the blade keen during regular stops to stretch and straighten the back.

3. Get in amongst crops before too many weeds are visible. Have a really close look all the time. Annihilated weeds will soon shrivel to nothing in dry, sunny conditions.

4. Always clean tools after a session on the plot. Wipe the business end with an oily rag before storing the hoe for use another day.

APRIL WEEK 3

JOBS TO DO THIS WEEK

IN THE GREENHOUSE

- Pot on kale.
- If your cat enjoys the greenhouse as much as you do be sure to keep her off the shelves where seedlings are growing. Puss can accidentally cause chaos in her quest for a warm spot to curl up in.
- Re-sow recently planted seeds if the cat has knocked over pots.
- Pot on Ailsa Craig and Red Alert tomatoes.
- Pot on Long Black aubergine and tomatillo Verde.
- Pot on all surviving pepper plants.
- Keep up the nightly torchlight patrols for munching molluscs.
- Ventilate well.
- Sow Kelveden and Hestia dwarf runner beans, Borlotto Di Fuoco and Blue Lake climbing French beans, Aiguillon dwarf French bean.
- Keep seedlings moist but not wet.

ON THE PLOT

- Plant out Early Pak 7 tomatoes into big pots outside in a sunny position. Use glass cloches for extra protection.
- Make time to potter with a cup of tea (or something stronger).
- If there is little rain then water newly-sown rows of seeds carefully with a fine rose on the can.
- Erect runner bean poles.
- Be ready to throw horticultural fleece over newly planted-out crops if the forecast is for frost.
- Sow pot marigold seeds direct.
- Be vigilant for slugs and snails. An after-dark torchlight mooch could prove very useful in helping to control the blighters.
- Keep the hoe busy.
- Clear open ground of weeds in readiness for planting or sowing.
- Apply a manure mulch around the bases of Nine Star Perennial broccoli.
- Dig the last Jerusalem artichokes.
- Mow grass paths.

April   WEEK 4

Dwarf French Beans

Now is an ideal time for making indoor sowings of dwarf French beans. Why not have a go yourself? Try them on a well lit window-sill if you have no access to a greenhouse. Dwarf French beans form low growing bushes, are easy to cultivate, demand less water than runner beans, and produce delicious pods for eating whilst young. If harvested carefully, a little and often, supplies will be available throughout the latter half of the summer.

Dwarf French beans are available as numerous named varieties with their own individual virtues and qualities. Although I enjoy growing different ones each year, Purple Teepee remains a favourite. It produces massed bunches of tender, stringless, pencil-like, purple-podded crops. They turn green upon cooking and are hard to resist when steamed and served with a drizzle of olive oil and seasoning or tossed raw in salads.

With such prospects in mind simply push the easy-to-handle, kidney-shaped beans singly and snugly into small pots of compost 5cm deep and place them on a sunny shelf in the greenhouse. Kept moist but not wet, they grow surprisingly quickly, looping two handsome leaves up and out of the growing medium. The youngsters can be planted outside in rich, sunny soil in a month or so, at 20cm intervals.

Direct outdoor sowing is an option if greenhouse space is tight but, as these beans are not at all hardy, this must be resisted until after all threats of frost have passed. Dwarf French beans will deliver worthwhile crops even if sown as late as the end of June.

In the first few weeks of their lives, plants will need some protection from slugs and snails if disappointment is to be avoided. Although I tolerate these admirable veg-eating blighters most of the time, I do do battle with them on two fronts during spring and early summer. Firstly, I make nightly torchlight forays into the garden and greenhouse to remove them by hand-picking (actually an extremely effective tactic). Secondly, I set beer traps strategically in sensitive areas. Beer-filled dishes are irresistible to the big-footed crop munchers, who slip-slide into them and drown.

APRIL Week 4: SOWING CLIMBING FRENCH BEANS

1. Fill twelve 9cm pots with peat-free multipurpose compost and set out in plastic fruit tray for ease of handling.

2. With forefinger, poke a 5cm hole and pop in one bean per pot. Tap sides to settle and level compost.

3. Magic added ingredient: a dribble of water from a small can. Use thumb to control the flow.

4. Don't forget to label and date your charges so you know what's what! Kept moist and warm, beans should be cracking the surface in a few days.

Tending Figs

This is also a good time for tending a fig tree. I planted my Brown Turkey variety about this time last year in a lined hole to restrict the roots and positioned it against a southwest facing wall for training into a fan. Kept well watered but not enriched, in that first summer the fig grew strongly. Good lengths of stem and a number of young embryo figlets were produced. I took the precaution of wrapping my tree in horticultural fleece for over-wintering protection against the worst of the weather. Fig husbandry for this week involved removing this swaddling now that the threat is diminished.

However, during a bout of extremely harsh early-spring conditions, the fig tree was subject to the unwanted attentions of visiting badgers. One or more Billies had ripped the fleece open and picked off the acorn-sized fruits. More than that, the two young shoots I had selected to form the fan framework had been gnawed down almost to the fork. Chuckling politely, Mrs Nails could hardly contain herself. With rolling eyes and knowing look she said, 'Well, what do you expect?' Apparently it is my own fault, having encouraged these black and white beasts into the garden in the first place.

Despite feeling alarm, distress and resigned amusement all at the same time, I'm far from

APRIL WEEK 4
JOBS TO DO THIS WEEK

IN THE GREENHOUSE

- Conduct consistent nightly torchlight slug and snail patrols.
- Ventilate well.
- Keep up with the watering.
- Set beer traps amongst pots and trays to control molluscs.
- Pot on lettuce seedlings.
- Pot on Nero di Toscana kale.
- Thin out carrots sown in pots earlier.

ON THE PLOT

- Un-swaddle Brown Turkey fig.
- Hoe onions, Jerusalem artichokes and all open ground
  (to keep it free of weeds and fit for cultivation).
- Plant Mange Tout peas.
- Prepare seed beds.
- Set beer traps amongst salads, tomatoes and cabbages.
- Plant out Rucola Coltivata rocket and Rhubarb Swiss chard.
- Adjust and tend to Feltham First Early peas trying to get a grip up their supports.
- Erect supports for Greenshaft and Mange Tout peas.
- Sow Nantes 2 carrots.
- Clear and compost spent salsify and scorzonera plants.
- Erect canes for climbing French beans.
- Keep trimming and tidying plot edges.
- Clear and compost exhausted purple sprouting and kale plants
  which have cropped well.
- Hand weed and hoe.

disheartened. As a wildlife-loving gardener, having this ongoing dialogue with the badgers via their nocturnal activities in and around the veg patch is as exciting and fulfilling as any potential crop of exquisite-tasting figs.

I snipped the ragged, chewed twig-ends clean off just above a healthy bud and am left with a tree that, although stunted, is still very much alive. Next on my list of jobs to do is to figure out how to protect it in the future.

April
Veg on the Menu

Leaves and greens
Kale
Nine Star Perennial broccoli
Purple sprouting broccoli

Roots, tubers and stems
Carrots
Jerusalem artichoke
Radish, French Breakfast
Scorzonera

Salads
Corn salad
Lettuce, Salad Bowl
Winter purslane

Onion tribe
Garlic (store)
Leek
Shallot (store)

Edible flowers
Salsify

Weeds
Stinging nettle tips

May

WEEK 1

Forget-me-nots

This week I have been admiring my wife's forget-me-nots. Her borders are alive with a massed, low-growing, pale-blue haze of these delightful flowers. Clusters of frothy blooms, made up of many five-petalled individuals, are borne at the end of branched stalks. Dancing and quaking in response to a gentle breeze, they reflect the amazing colour of a cloudless summer sky, each with a yellow sun at its heart. Bathed in sunshine during the daytime, their beauty is as enchanting as it is modest and understated.

Come the late evening, when light is failing fast and the garden enters that hinter-world between day and night, forget-me-nots radiate a magical luminous glow. It is enough to make the existence of fairies seem a distinct possibility.

They will flower in abundance given half a chance. Mrs Nails ensures a lovely display every late-April/early-May by up-rooting armfuls of the plants just at the point when they have turned and are on the wane. She hangs the gathered bunches, tied with string, in a sheltered place and waits for the developing seeds to ripen. When they have dried and turned brown she strolls around the garden with them, shaking seeds over places where she wants them to grow next season. They scatter freely, some germinating before the summer is out but the bulk emerging early the following spring.

Her tactics clear the flower beds of forget-me-nots when they are looking tatty and beyond their best. They also create spaces and gaps for other plants to spread themselves in to, allowing for a succession of summer shapes and colours.

Baby Blackbirds

The antics of newly-fledged blackbirds can cause concern at this time of the year. A neighbour came calling when I was down the allotment at the weekend. She was worried about a couple of youngsters that were flapping about in her garden.

The question was, with cats in the area, what to do? Consulting with knowledgeable pals who were working their plot next door, the answer came back that in this situation the only sensible tactic is to try and keep the felines away and let mum (who will be close by and watchful) sort them out until they can get a takeoff and find a safe place to perch. While on the ground, fledgling blackies are vulnerable, so bushes and other cover is important at this make-or-break time. It is best not to move them because the bond with parents will be broken.

Fresh out of the nest, blackbirds are poor fliers, with no prominent tail feathers and a dull beak. Leaving alone can be a hard thing to do, especially when danger is so obviously all around. But these birds are survivors. Even if the current brood is lost, Mrs Blackbird will already be thinking about raising her next batch of youngsters.

Nettle Soup

Whilst visiting friends a few days ago I was delighted to be served up with a bowl of nettle soup. The startlingly bright-green dish had real body and vitality. It was thin but not at all watery and thoroughly more-ish in every respect. One of my mates, thrilled with his culinary concoction, was very happy to share the recipe and methods, adding that this soup is very quick and easy to rustle up.

DEREK'S NETTLE SOUP

Ingredients
1 bucket (about 250) stinging nettle tips
2 large red onions
Several cloves of garlic to taste
1 litre of vegetable stock
Drizzle of olive oil
Seasoning

Method
Wearing kitchen gloves and using scissors, harvest the tender nettle tips before any flower buds are forming. Wash in cold water. Drizzle a drop of olive oil into a saucepan, add the peeled and chopped onions and garlic, sweating until soft without browning. Then pour in the stock, bring to boiling point, and tip in the nettles. Compress and stir with a wooden spoon before allowing to simmer for 5 minutes (it is this heat which takes the sting out of nettles). Blend and serve with black pepper, grated nutmeg and the juice of half a lemon as optional extras.

A continuous supply of this nutritious and delicious wild food can be ensured by cutting nettles down every few weeks, thus stimulating constant fresh re-growth. Stingers exceed spinach as a source of iron, are rich in many essential dietary elements and provide generous portions of Vitamin C to help ward off spring colds.

MAY Week 1: SOWING SWEDES

1. Use a finger to make holes 2cm deep and 15cm apart. 'Station sow' three seeds per hole. Thin to the strongest seedling in 20 days or so.

2. Alternatively, swedes can be sown in a 2cm deep furrow or 'drill'. Not long after they emerge removing alternate and/or weak specimens will give choice seedlings room to develop.

3. Kept moist and weed free, swedes grow vigorously. Further thinning will be needed in a few weeks to allow final spacings of about 30cm between plants.

4. Swedes swell up and provide a heavy yield of cream and purple skinned, deep yellow fleshed portions from October onwards. Very hardy vegetables, swedes can be left in the ground as a 'standing crop' until needed.

MAY WEEK 1
JOBS TO DO THIS WEEK

IN THE GREENHOUSE

- Ventilate.
- Conduct nightly torchlight slug and snail patrols.
- Monitor watering demands of seedlings and developing crops in pots.
- Pot on kale and cabbages.
- Rearrange shelving and positioning of pots to accommodate setting up of growing-bags with Tumbler tomatoes planted into them.

ON THE PLOT

- Cut out flower spikes if they start to issue forth from the middle of rhubarb crowns.
- Sow Rocula Coltivata rocket and French Breakfast radish direct.
- Mow all grass paths.
- Trim the edges with long-handled edging irons.
- Sow Marian swede.
- Look for slugs amongst seedlings by torchlight and evict them.
- Amble around with a cup of tea and caretaker's eye to check all is well on the plot.
- Plant out Red Alert and Ailsa Craig tomatoes in a sunny and sheltered bed.
- Keep the hoe busy whenever the sun shines and you have a moment or three to spare.
- Plant out Brussels sprout plants.
- Hand weed amongst the peas.
- Clean out dirty water butts and refill.
- Apply a generous watering to all young fruit trees: a bucket each is good.
- Water spuds, chard, broad beans and radishes if rain is not forthcoming.
- Remove cloches from protected salads and lettuces so you can get in amongst them for a thorough weeding session.
- Where Tardel beetroot, spring onions and carrots have failed (yes, it does happen!) prepare the ground to try again.
- Plant out True Gold and Kelvedon sweetcorn in a sunny spot with cloche protection.
- When the broad beans are blooming water regularly to encourage plenty of fat pods.
- Plant out Roxton leeks for midsummer consumption as babies.
- Sow Tardel and Cylindra beetroot after clearing exhausted kale.
- Clear exhausted cabbage plants, weed, hoe and rake soil to a fine and level tilth.

May

Asparagus

It is important to keep an asparagus bed completely free of weeds at all times. Unwanted plants that become rooted deeply and established will compete with your intended crop for moisture and nutrients so must be removed at the earliest opportunity whilst still young and small. Digging out invaders is not an option because damage will be done to the asparagus roots. Hoeing is detrimental too, as emerging shoots can be just below the surface and are vulnerable to a sharp hoe blade. Hand weeding is the only option at this stage and, painstaking though it is, it must be done.

I'd recommend getting amongst your rows of asparagus this week, on hands and knees with head down. In the sunshine, tiddler weed seedlings can simply be left on top with their roots exposed, to shrivel in the heat. Personally I thoroughly enjoy weeding. It's a pleasant job when undertaken on a calm morning, with surround-sound birdsong providing a feast for the ears.

Shoots emerging from an asparagus bed prepared and planted up over the last winter and spring should be allowed to develop unhindered and absolutely nothing must be taken by way of a crop. The underground 'crowns' need to grow over the next few months and then re-absorb the goodness which they generate themselves in order to become strong and established.

A first-year bed requires only to be kept weed free at this stage. It is the same for second-year beds. Only when into the third year may a small harvest be taken, so as not to exhaust the plants.

Happily for my friends and family I have been patiently working on and waiting for my bed to get beyond these formative years. Cutting quantities of the delicious phallic spears commenced in the last few days. This involves using a sharp knife to sever the length about 2.5cm deep when it is finger-thick and no more than 25cm long. The season is short, coming to a close around mid-June, so we intend to enjoy it while it lasts. Mrs Nails agrees that there is nothing finer than fresh, steamed asparagus, taken simply with a drizzle of olive oil and a shake 'n' twist of salt 'n' pepper.

House Martins

The house martins are back, entertaining the neighbourhood with their aerial antics and friendly, bubbling calls. Towards the end of the week, a good friend from down the road knocked on the door with the fantastic news: both her house martin nests have residents who arrived that morning.

Pulling on some loosely laced boots, I scuffed along the street to take a look. Rena and husband Peter, about to leave for somewhere in the car, were beaming like proud parents. The little birds had just that second flown in and we all watched in anticipation. A moment later, in the blink of an eye, a black-and-white flash as a house martin dropped out and took to the wing. Half a dozen of them skimmed above the rooftops, arching and soaring in the sky. We were overjoyed to see them back in their summer home.

MAY Week 2: WEEDS (1)

1. WILDLIFE FRIENDLY: attract beneficial insects for pollination purposes or to control pests naturally. White deadnettle has clusters of flask-shaped hooded flowers, especially adapted for easy nectar collection by bumble bees. Their pollinating activities are crucial for producing bumper bean and pea crops.

2. EPHEMERAL (or 'RUDERAL'): very short lived. Pioneering plants among the first to colonise open soil. Often produce several generations in one season. Hairy bitter cress spills on average 600 seeds per plant every few weeks.

3. ANNUAL: adapted to grow, set seed and die in one season. Cannot survive the cold of British winters. Cleavers (goose grass or sticky-buds) remain dormant over the long, cold months as seeds in the soil.

4. PERENNIAL: flowers that persist from year to year. Slower growing, surviving one year to the next from food and moisture reserves gathered in thick, fleshy roots. Daisies stash winter supplies in rubbery, fibrous roots.

JOBS TO DO THIS WEEK

IN THE GREENHOUSE
- Ventilate well.
- Water daily.
- Plant Tumbler tomatoes into growing-bags.
- Prick out earlier sowings of Prinz and Mars celeriac into individual pots.
- Make another sowing of celeriac as insurance.
- Pot on tomatillo Verde.
- Every evening after dark search for slugs and snail by torchlight.

ON THE PLOT
- Check all crops with regard to their state of health, watering needs and for signs of pests and diseases.
- Thin out carrots sown in pots.
- Hand weed potatoes.
- Hoe between rows of developing veggies and open ground to keep weeds at bay.
- Hand weed garlic, shallots, leek nursery and asparagus bed.
- Water swedes to jolly them along and keep flea beetle damage to a minimum (they love to munch holes in the leaves, especially when the ground is dry).
- Sow spring onions.
- Plant out Tiger lettuces.
- Use young Witkiem broad bean plants, sown as extras at the end of the row, to fill in gaps where plants have failed for some reason or seeds not germinated.
- Sow Boltardy beetroot.
- Hoe and hand weed maincrop onions to keep the crop really clean.
- Prepare a new bed for kale: clean, enrich, turn and firm.
- Plant out Pentland Brig and Habholer Grun Krausner kale.
- Dig out 'volunteer' overlooked Jerusalem artichokes from last year's planting position to make room for something else.
- Get into the shed and keep it tidy in there!
- Prepare a bed for dwarf French beans.
- Plant out Kelvedon runner beans, Blue Lake climbing French beans and Augillion dwarf French beans.
- Mow all grass paths and trim the edges.

May   WEEK 3

Pricking out Celeriac

This week the time is about right for pricking-out celeriac seedlings from seed tray into small individual pots. Turnip-rooted celery, as it is alternatively known, is a notoriously slow developer in the early days. From a sowing made in the fourth week of March they are delicate, with little maple-shaped leaves emerging from between two opposite, long, oval, seed leaves. I think it's a good idea to nurture tender seedlings in a protected environment until early-June if you can. Then, when the weather is lovely they can romp away in their final resting places with leaps and bounds.

In the meantime, prepare your pots by filling to just below the rim with suitable compost (multi-purpose or John Innes Number 1) and pushing a hole centrally with the end of your finger. Then use a 'widger' (small, flattened tool; a round-ended kitchen knife or lolly-stick is perfect) to ease the celeriac seedlings out of the tray, complete with their stringy, fibrous dangle of thin roots. With the softest of touches, one at a time, lower each plant down into the hole (one per pot) so as to keep the seedling leaves slightly proud of the compost when it is gently firmed around.

MAY Week 3: PLANTING OUT CLIMBING FRENCH BEANS

1. Climbing French beans thrive from seeds sown in pots during April. In less than a month, showing two sets of leaves and lolling around like unruly teenagers, they are ready for planting out on the plot.

2. They need to climb by spiralling up a supporting framework. Parallel rows of canes are traditional, but a square of four rods pushed in 30cm apart and lashed together at the top is easy and quick.

3. Scoop a hole in fertile soil large enough to accommodate the root-ball easily. Slip the beans from their pots with compost and roots intact. Place carefully in the hole and back-fill, firming gently.

4. Training is essential until the beans get themselves going. String can be used, but must be very loosely tied so as not to damage tender stems. There is little else to do except keep moist, weed-free and wait with eager anticipation.

Making a Wormery

Cooked vegetable matter and other food waste is unsuitable for depositing on the compost heap as the addition of this stuff can be attractive to rats. A worm-composting bin, or 'wormery', is ideal for hygienically disposing of this and processed kitchen waste. Wormeries can be purchased as a proprietary product or cobbled together at home.

Mine are home-made jobs, constructed by using an old water butt for starters. A small-gauge wire mesh 'sieve' sits on a bed of rocks and crocks at the bottom, just above the level of the all-important drainage tap. This acts as a sink for collecting fluids and juices. In turn, these will make an excellent liquid fertiliser to dilute with water for direct application to growing crops. On top of the sieve lies a thick bed of damp straw (shredded newspaper will do fine), and then a 5cm layer of horse manure.

For worms (the all-important active ingredient) the simplest (and most fun!) thing to do is simply pick through a bag or two of rotting manure which has been kept handy for other jobs. They are generally teeming with red 'brandling' and striped 'tiger' worms, who are the best chaps to use for the task of transforming biodegradable household refuse into dark, crumbly, sweet-smelling, nutrient-rich compost. 200 or so of the hard-working wrigglers placed in the wormery at this stage will get it going nicely. The only thing to do

then is add waste in layers of not more than 15cm at a time, replace the bin lid, and leave the worms to commence weaving their magic before adding some more.

Temperatures below 15 degrees centigrade are not conducive to worm activity, so the set-up must be given protection in the winter. When the wormery is full of compost, a proportion of the worms can be extracted and set to work on the next culture.

MAY WEEK 3

JOBS TO DO THIS WEEK

IN THE GREENHOUSE

- Water daily.
- Slug and snail patrols nightly.
- Pot on red cabbage then place outside.
- Sow American land cress in trays.

ON THE PLOT

- Plant out various lettuces amongst the Brussels sprouts as a 'catch crop'.
- Earth up First Early potatoes.
- Tidy and weed strawberries in containers.
- Plant out Nero di Toscana, Westland Winter and Pentland Brig kale.
- Plant out strapping young pot grown sunflowers.
- Plant out pot marigolds along plot edges for a decorative and edible wildlife-friendly border.
- Put supports around burgeoning broad beans: use a cane at each corner and lash string around the whole lot at the top, middle and bottom.
- Cut down grasses and weeds around soft fruit bushes and amongst apples and pears.
- Hand weed around globe artichoke crowns.
- Stuff nettles and comfrey into an old wormery bin to make home-made liquid fertiliser.
- Collect manure in old compost bags and deliver to the plot. Store for future use.
- Mow all grass paths and trim plot edges.
- Make a wormery to take cooked kitchen waste.
- Use shears to tame rank grasses and weeds around the compost bins.
- Sweep concrete paths.
- Harvest Nine Star perennial broccoli.
- Plant Carentan 3 leeks into a nursery bed.
- Potter and mooch morning and night.
- Tie in outdoor tomatoes to supporting canes and pinch out growth from between leaf node and stem.
- Check supports for peas are adequate as the heavy crop swells.
- Plant out Mini Pop sweetcorn.
- Apply supporting strings and canes for Witkiem broad beans.
- Pot on January King cabbages.
- Earth up Second Early and Maincrop spuds.

May

Hazel

Whilst visiting my local garden centre at the weekend I picked up a couple of surplus hazel 'whips' (young, single-stemmed trees with no branches) which were left over from a hedging job and the manager was happy to let go for free. I set out for the back of the veg plot immediately on getting home. Allowing 90cm between plants, the bare-rooted youngsters were plonked into a wild corner by simply opening a slit in the soil with a spade, pushing the roots down and in, then stamping firm all around. They look a bit neglected and sorry for themselves now but should take okay if given plenty of water and tender loving care throughout the summertime. Really, the tree-planting season is over. If needs must at this time of year, a pot-grown specimen is the best bet in terms of successful cultivation. November to March is better for bare-rooters, when they are more or less dormant. This, however, was one of those occasions when the 'rules' needed to be broken.

When planning to include any tree in the garden, the minimum distance that it should be planted away from the house is no less than half the expected mature height. For example, an eventual 15 metre individual needs to be at least 7.5 metres away.

Hazel has a multitude of uses in the garden as pea sticks, bean poles and for the type of artisan creations that Mrs Nails likes to weave in and amongst her climbers and flower borders. The practice of cutting hazel to the ground every few years, known as 'coppicing', yields such garden essentials. Hazel products don't last as long as bamboo (just one or two years tops), but they can be easily and sustainably produced every year or three at no cost by simply cultivating a couple somewhere out of the way. Hazels are naturally trees of the woodland under-storey so quite content to do their thing in partial shade.

Sycamore

There are many opinions as to the virtues, or not, of the sycamore tree. To some it is a weed species, to others a handsome, valuable addition to the town and country environment. Certainly its rapid growth when young and tolerance of polluted or salt-laden air make it an ideal choice for urban or coastal areas. Sycamores respond handsomely when their size is managed by coppicing or 'pollarding' (cut off some way above the ground, traditionally above livestock- or deer-grazing height), and useful in much the same way as hazel, if a little less versatile.

It is out in open countryside and parklands where the true grandeur of this tree can be fully appreciated. With a massive domed outline potentially reaching 35 metres in height, akin to the shapely form of an English elm (sadly, mostly now a thing of the past in our landscape), I think it is worth making every effort to view sycamores where they have room for unfettered growth. One benefit the Great Plane (as it is alternatively known) has for wildlife in May is the wealth of insects that are attracted to its greening bosom by the freshly unfolded, hand-shaped ('palmate') leaves and dangling green garlands of flowers which modestly adorn by the tens of thousands in the early summer.

I spent a glorious lunchtime half hour at the edge of town mid-week, sheltered beneath the canopy of one of these giant hedgerow sentinels. It was about to rain and I was watching massed flocks of twittering, bubbling, mischievously chattering house martins and swallows that exploded from within and around the treetops, feasting on the huge reservoirs of insect food attracted to the vicinity of these tall trees. This bounty of invertebrate protein is crucial to such birds early in their breeding season.

Against a darkened backdrop of banks of thick cloud approaching, the black and white martins twisted and curved in a dazzling, mazy, feeding-frenzied dance, swirling in response to the movement of their food and the buffeting of a pre-shower, strengthening breeze. Swallows dashed and weaved lower down, jewels of flashing, streamer'd blue, trawling for morsels that dwell just above ground height, like well-aimed and well-thrown pebbles skimming the surface of a pond.

MAY Week 4: COMFREY

   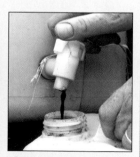

1. Easy-to-grow comfrey is attractive to bees and other beneficial insects. Cultivating comfrey in a corner of the garden is helpful to wildlife and useful to the gardener too.

2. Cut the comfrey to ground level with shears. Load leaves, stems and flowers into a wheelbarrow for ease of transportation. Comfrey can irritate the skin, so a garden fork may prove helpful.

3. Cram everything into an old wormery bin. There is no need to add water. Chomp the comfrey cuttings down with shears if they are spilling over the edges.

4. After a few weeks drain the rich liquid fertiliser into a container. A drop stirred into a 10 litre watering can provides a great once-weekly feed for veggies.

MAY WEEK 4
JOBS TO DO THIS WEEK

IN THE GREENHOUSE
- Check tomatoes and other crops daily for pests and diseases and also watering needs.
- Ventilate freely.
- Check for slugs and snails every night by torchlight.
- Pinch out aubergine side shoots and tie in to supporting canes.
- Sow Salad Bowl lettuce.
- Place cucumbers and squashes outside to harden off with protection at night.

ON THE PLOT
- Wash empty pots.
- Check over all areas.
- More weeding around globe artichoke crowns.
- Pinch out outdoor tomatoes.
- Plant dill seedlings amongst sweetcorn.
- Plant camomile seedlings under step-over apples at path edges.
- Plant out lettuces.
- Tie in new growth of Wagener, Pixie and Merton Knave step-over apples.
- If the weather is very wet then erect some kind of tent-like shelter over outdoor tomatoes to save them from getting wrecked.
- Set slug traps with beer.
- Plant out pot marigolds.
- Let plot borders grow wild for the creatures who like these places but keep on top of areas which are near important areas like the water butt (it's no fun getting stung whilst fetching a pail of water).
- Insert stout supports for sweetcorn plants.
- Plant out courgettes.
- Weed plot edges.
- Mow grass paths and trim edges.
- Compost spent purple sprouting broccoli.
- Plant out Butternut Waltham, Marina di Chioggia and Uchiki Kuri squash.
- Check and tend Brussels sprouts.
- Transplant red lettuces.
- Thin carrots.

May

Snow in May

With lacy platters of cow parsley just past their best and waning, the countryside is given a fresh breath of life at this time of year by an array of summer-blooming, woody plants. One of the late-May/June highlights comes when hawthorn (or 'quick thorn') is in full flower. Taking a spin out in the motor with Mrs Nails reveals a picture-postcard landscape alive with specimens of this common hedgerow dweller, densely plastered with creamy white blossom. The air, too, becomes heady with a distinctive, sickly-sweet aroma. In a good year one could be forgiven for believing that snow has fallen in May, so heavy and billowing are the lanes and byways with frothy hawthorn blooms.

Now is the perfect time to see them in their full decorative glory, feel inspired, and make plans for incorporating this species come the planting season in winter. Also known as 'Maythorn', it is an ideal choice to cultivate in the garden. It is modest of growth and accommodating to the needs of most domestic spaces be they large, small, sunny or partially shaded.

Planted in lines to make a hedge, hawthorn is second to none. Once established, it will thrive whether kept in trim with shears or a hedge cutter, laid as a prickly stock- or child-proof barrier every few years, or allowed to develop unkempt and unchecked. Hawthorn will actually become a splendid medium-sized tree if granted the room with a wonderfully fulsome, cascading form that can attain heights of up to 14 metres. However, pruning will temper the 'Mayflower' considerably so that, as a bush, it can be maintained to almost any size or shape of choosing.

Hawthorns combine enormous ornamental and wildlife values. The common variety is a stunner in its own right but alternatives are available. Rosa Pleno-flore and Paul's Scarlet are a little less vigorous, single or double, pink- or red-flowered hybrids. They look spectacular in a garden where space is at a premium. A host of insects rely on this thorn for food and shelter. These in turn support all manner of birds and wild creatures. Come autumn, the boughs will be ablaze with bright clusters of red berries. This sight for sore eyes can be painstakingly harvested to make a wild jam rich in Vitamin C or left to provide essential winter sustenance for the thrushes, blackbirds and others.

An abiding childhood memory of mine is seeing great 'tents' full of lackey moth caterpillars slung between branches of hawthorns up Landsdown Road on the walk to school. I'd watch my older brother collect some every year. Big bro' would nurture the fascinating blue-grey headed, red, white and blue-striped hairy caterpillars in customised ice-cream tubs. After undergoing a series of moults (or 'instars'), they developed into cocoons and were released from whence they came.

Snow in May continued

Horticulturally speaking, lackey moths are bad guys because, when immature, they can defoliate trees including apples and pears. But I would be quite happy to see a ghost-like, silken purse full of the critters in the vicinity of my plot, potential damage not withstanding, for the sheer thrill of seeing natural life being lived.

Bean Weevils

The leaves of broad beans are often punctuated by small, semi-circular notches cut out from the leaf margins as spring slips into summer. This is the work of adult bean weevils. They are small, grey-brown beetles up to 4 mm long. There is no need for being concerned by their leaf-cutting habits. A healthy crop of well developed broads will happily tolerate the nibbling attentions of these weevils with no loss of produce. As grubs, bean weevils live in the soil, quietly and harmlessly feeding on the nitrogen-fixing nodules which are a feature of legumes (peas and beans).

MAY Week 5: PLANTING OUT PURPLE SPROUTING BROCCOLI

1. Prepare a bed which is weed-free and can accommodate each plant with 60cm growing space all around. Dig a hole twice as big and deep as the pot your purple sprouting youngster is in.

2. Flop a couple of handfuls of well-rotted manure or compost into the hole. Purple sprouting is a hungry plant and will appreciate the extra goodness. If conditions are dry, fill with water then allow to drain.

3. Supporting the stem between first two fingers, invert the pot. Tap the bottom and slide pot free. Healthy specimens show a well-developed network of creamy-white roots. Plant deep with the lowest leaves just above soil level. Firm with your heel.

4. To keep destructive root-eating Cabbage Root Fly maggots at bay, fit 10cm squares of carpet underlay around the stem at soil level. Cut a slit and notch to slide in snugly but not too tight.

MAY WEEK 5

JOBS TO DO THIS WEEK

IN THE GREENHOUSE

- Check over and ventilate daily.
- Water tomatoes and other crops every day.

ON THE PLOT

- Plant out Spaghetti squash.
- Replenish slug and snail beer traps.
- Tie urine-soaked rags up around sweetcorn to dissuade badgers (they find this crop irresistible and just can't stop helping themselves!).
- Trim and weed plot edges.
- Mow all grass paths.
- Cut back and compost stinging nettles where they are in the wrong place.
- Hoe amongst beetroot.
- Keep a fleece handy to sling over tender squashes, beans and courgettes if a late frost is forecast.
- Trim honeysuckle growing over the shed.
- Tie in Loch Ness thornless blackberry.
- Tidy and potter.
- Plant out corn salad seedlings.
- Keep the hoe busy everywhere.
- Earth up spuds as and when the tops have grown sufficiently for this to seem necessary.
- Plant out tomatillo Verde.
- Give water to various crops if the weather is sustained dry, especially broad beans in flower.
- Plant Aiguillion dwarf French beans direct.
- Have a summer bonfire with young friends and neighbours after a session watering and weeding on the plot to inspire their interest in gardening and the great outdoors.
- Hand weed asparagus bed.
- Plant Kelvedon runner beans direct to make up for any nipped by frost.
- Collect manure from common land with youngsters to show them the magical life in piles of pooh!
- Remove covering from outdoor tomatoes when it seems that summer has really arrived.
- Show zero tolerance to weeds and certainly don't let them set seed.
- Plant out red cabbages.

May
Veg on the Menu

Leaves and greens
Broccoli, Nine Star Perennial
Cleavers (Goosegrass)
Purple sprouting broccoli
Stinging nettles
Swiss chard

Roots, tubers and stems
Asparagus
Radish, French Breakfast
Rhubarb

Salads
Corn salad
Lettuce, Dynamite, Lobjoits
Green Cos, Salad Bowl
Nasturtium
Winter purslane

Peas and beans
Broad beans

Onion tribe
Chives
Garlic
Onion, winter Radar
Shallots

Edible flowers
Salsify

Fughi
Cultivated mushroom

June

WEEK 1

French Beans

Dwarf and climbing French beans can be safely sown direct at this time of year. The soil is lovely and warm to the touch and getting them in now will ensure a flying start. I've been out on the plot planting these beans with my nephew. The young lad is not naturally drawn to gardening at home but is a grand little helper with outside chores and tasks when visiting his old Uncle!

Beans are irresistible, solid, smooth and shiny. They have a certain magic which is almost tangible when a dozen or so are cradled in the palm. These are easy plants to grow and great to handle whether you are a ten-year old novice with soft clean hands, much older and slightly less nimble-fingered, or somewhere in-between.

Climbing variety Barlotta Lingua Di Fuocci seeds are 2cm long, plump, light-brown with darker streaks and marbling. The pods can be steamed whole or left on the vine to dry out, then harvested, shelled and stored for winter use. Blue Lake is another popular climber, producing tender, stringless, pencil-like pods. The beans are half the size of Barlotta and ivory-white. Dwarf variety Aiguillon will produce bountiful masses of delicious food so long as the young stringless pods continue to be gathered from the low-growing, bushy plants. The elegant beans are dark and slender with a white eye, or 'hilum' (the point of attachment to the mother pod).

French beans require 20cm between plants. They can simply be pushed into prepared ground that has been enriched, dug over and raked to a level tilth. 5cm is a good depth. I instructed my nephew to push the beans down in pairs for subsequent thinning to the strongest one shortly after they have emerged.

A combination of moisture (via rain or the watering-can) and hot summer sun will get these vigorous growers jumping up out of the ground in a matter of days. Batches sown in early-June will complement earlier greenhouse sowings made about mid-April and planted outside after May 12th (or a fortnight later in the North). Such succession-sowing should extend the cropping season considerably.

Cylinder mowers & Slow Worms

Grass cutting continues to be a job that needs to be done regularly. For the small lawn, a manually operated cylinder mower is perfect. They are light, easy to handle and do a top-notch job. These little machines are cheap to buy, simple and safe for the user to operate. There is no risk of cutting electric cables and no fuel to pay for and then burn. They need only to be given a drop of oil to moving parts every now and then and be sharpened once in a blue moon. Manual cylinder mowers are quiet, so won't disturb the neighbours on a Sunday morning, with the bonus of providing a satisfying and relaxing way of taking exercise.

All cutting jobs have the potential to harm beneficial creatures in the garden. Frogs and toads are annually wiped out in their thousands by mowers and strimmers as an unfortunate, accidental by-product of the gardener's desire for neat and tidy clipped grass. I was extremely upset earlier in the week to slice a slow worm in half whilst tending the paths around my patch. Dangerously, these garden and allotment residents like to bask in sun-kissed spots. Short grass on south-facing slopes is ideal.

In spite of their snake-like appearance, slow worms are in fact legless lizards and totally harmless to humans. A large specimen may be finger-thick and 20cm in length, but they are commonly half that size. Their skin is fairly uniform in colour, ranging from brown-gold through to silver-grey. Although it is made up of tiny scales, it is silky-smooth to the touch. If startled, a slow-worm will glide effortlessly into the thick sward. Their favourite food is slugs, which are consumed in vast quantities from the moment they are born.

The fatality occurred because I was in a rush and didn't carry out my usual wildlife-friendly routine of slowly walking through the area to be dealt with immediately before-hand, to give pest-eating critters a chance to slither, hop, or steal away into safety.

June Week 1: BLACKFLY ON BROAD BEANS

1. Blackfly can devastate a crop at this time of year. These sap-sucking pests may descend and extract the life out of beans as they form. Autumn-sown varieties such as Aquadulce (above) are less prone to attack than spring-sown broads which are younger and more tender.

2. Affected areas can be sprayed with a weak solution of biodegradable washing-up liquid and water dispensed through a hand-held mist sprayer.

3. Tender tips can be physically pinched out and composted or burnt. If removed before infestation occurs, these portions can be steamed and eaten as delicious greens.

4. Not interfering with the natural prey/predator balance in your garden allows beneficial creatures such as ladybirds to thrive. They gorge themselves on blackfly and will soon have the problem under control in a totally environmentally-friendly manner.

JUNE WEEK 1
JOBS TO DO THIS WEEK

IN THE GREENHOUSE
- Ventilate freely.
- Water crops daily.
- Check for signs of pests and disease.
- Prick out celeriac seedlings.

ON THE PLOT
- Keep the hoe busy, a little and often every day.
- Water beetroot seedlings, squashes and kale.
- Check over spuds and parsnips for signs of badger damage.
- Plant out purple sprouting broccoli.
- Hand weed and hoe amongst carrots.
- Harvest and hang winter Radar onions.
- Hand weed here and there.
- Replant rows of carrots where germination has failed or seedlings have been taken by slugs.
- Liquid feed dwarf French beans.
- Sprinkle light dusting of calcium on onion bed (bare) in preparation for cabbages to follow.
- Plant out January King cabbages.
- Water beans and peas, artichokes and cucurbits with a little liquid feed added if you fancy.
- Pinch out side ('adventitious') shoots from tomatoes.
- Plant out Salad Bowl lettuce.
- Keep tomatillos and cucumbers watered and weed-free.
- Thin and weed beetroot seedlings.
- Hand weed asparagus bed.
- Thoroughly examine asparagus for beetles. Hand pick and destroy if found.
- Sow Chevalier calibrese.
- Tie in outdoor tomatoes to supporting canes.
- Weed baby leek nursery bed.
- Weed and trim plot edges.
- Mow grass paths.
- Cut and compost comfrey.
- Plant out Marketmore cucumber.

June

Planting out Celeriac

This is the week for planting out carefully nurtured celeriac plants. Seeds were sown in March, the resulting seedlings carefully pricked out and potted on come mid-May. Kept moist and warm in the greenhouse they've made slow but steady progress, becoming sturdy little specimens with extensive root systems filling their pots. By now, mid-June, they are demanding a sunny spot on the plot.

Celeriac will be harvested throughout the winter months, having developed a pock-marked, cricket ball-sized swollen stem over the summer months. It can be steamed or eaten raw, either grated or in chip-shaped chunks. The taste is of mild celery, clean in the mouth and long-lasting. The leaves are available to be taken separately throughout this time and make a flavoursome addition to soups. It is always a treat for Mrs Nails in those cold, dark months, when I arrive filthy dirty at the back door and announce that a celeriac has been lifted and cleaned in preparation for dinner.

To thrive, this vegetable prefers a rich soil kept moist. It's a good idea to prepare the ground by thoroughly removing all weeds and forking in a little garden compost if needed. Having raked to a level, crumbly tilth, mark out the rows with canes and string. Then, using a swan-

JUNE Week 2: PLANTING OUT LEEKS

1. Lift young, pencil-thick leeks from nursery bed. Keep them in water-filled bucket for immediate transplanting to final resting places.

2. Use a broken spade handle with rounded-off end, or purpose-bought dibber, to make planting holes 15cm deep at 15cm intervals.

3. Place one leek per hole. Stringy roots may need slight trimming with scissors. 'Puddle in' by filling each hole with water. Allow to drain naturally. Let soil settle over the next few days of its own accord.

4. Keep rows moist and weed-free. Growing different plants together can prove beneficial to both. Here, leeks have been 'companion planted' with dill.

necked (or 'draw') hoe, make a shallow flat-bottomed drill and put the little ones into this. Spacing them out at 30cm intervals is ideal, with 45cm between rows. This will afford plenty of room for each one to form an extensive network of gnarled roots.

At this stage it is important not to plant them too low down in the soil. To this end, pop them in only just deep enough to keep upright. Planting in this way makes watering easy because the sunken drill concentrates all drink to the roots, with no wasted run-off (especially useful if planted on a slope). Kept moist and weed-free, all being well, refreshing celeriac should be on the menu in a few months' time.

Fledgling Great Tits

In the last few days there has been much activity from the family of great tits nesting in a box on the end of our house. These birds raise one brood of youngsters in a season and, having worked tirelessly for the last twenty-odd days fetching and carrying about 15 thousand grubs and caterpillars to their growing babes, it was make or break time mid-week.

Mum and dad 'titmouse' called to the children from the branches of a big old apple tree a swoop away. They emitted urgent, scolding cries continuously. A crimson-chested bullfinch and posse of blue tits passed through as the drama unfolded. A newly-flown family of starlings, successfully raised in a neighbour's roof cavity, wafted between the top of a holly tree and nearby television aerials.

Then, after a short period of quiet, the calls changed. Great tits turned to whistling chimes and softer trills to beckon their full-grown chicks. One adult flitted amongst a tangle of honeysuckle around the box, dangling a tempting green caterpillar as incentive to fledge. With no joy, parents'

patience waned and relented as the juicy morsel was delivered through the box hole to a delighted crescendo of juvenile twittering chatter. Amongst the hullabaloo, anxious human observers could hear the fluttering of tiny wings from within, like holding a moth in your hands.

A relative calm had descended once more an hour or so later. The brood had refused to budge. Mum and dad were again on feeding duty, back and forth, but less frequently than before. Those dangerous moments when birds make their maiden voyage from the nest had been postponed for another time.

Mrs Nails and I have enjoyed witnessing the natural soap opera these last few weeks, from the initial checking out suitable nesting sites until now. In that time we've developed a rather parental emotional attachment. We were both sad to miss the moments of truth a day later. However, the sudden emptiness of that honeysuckle-clad wall and lack of tell-tale feathers in the area told the happy story of a successful mission accomplished.

JUNE WEEK 2
JOBS TO DO THIS WEEK

IN THE GREENHOUSE
- Ventilate freely.
- Water daily.
- Liquid feed established tomatoes, peppers and aubergines.
- Keep a keen eye for signs of pests and disease, and act appropriately

ON THE PLOT
- Mooch around the plot having a good look at the amazing world of vegetables, fruits and nature!
- Remove yellowing lower leaves from outdoor tomatoes.
- Plant out Pentland Brig kale and Rhodynda Red cabbage.
- Hoe over open soil and seedbeds to keep them ready for sowing and planting.
- Hoe through Brussels sprouts and lettuces.
- Water newly-planted January King cabbages and Mini Pop sweetcorn.
- Water strawberries in containers.
- Give every young fruit tree a bucket of water each if conditions are dry.
- Fix any leaky hoses immediately; don't leave these annoying jobs until tomorrow.
- Keep broad beans well watered as their pods swell.
- Secure stout posts either end of each asparagus row, then tie strings between to support feathery growth and prevent stems from snapping in summer storms.
- Sow seeds of a green manure crop on open ground which won't be used for raising crops this season.
- Trim all edges and keep them neat.
- Plant out celeriac.
- Plant out Chevalier calibrese and various kale seedlings.
- Hand weed wherever needed.
- Plant Tiger Cross marrows in amongst runner beans as a companion crop and to save space.
- Hand weed asparagus bed.
- Water thoroughly with a can if rain is scarce.
- Earth up all spuds.
- Check over crops and remove any sickly-looking foliage to maintain health and vigour.
- Thin beetroots again.
- Mow grass paths.
- Tie in and pinch out tomatoes.
- Tie in runner beans where needed.

June

Ground Elder (Goutweed)

This is as good a time as any for getting on your hands and knees and doing some serious weeding. I can often be found in a friend's flower border in June, patiently and meticulously extracting ground elder. This is a really invasive and persistent plant. Some would say that it is impossible to eradicate once established without recourse to the use of heavy-duty chemicals. However, happily for the soil and wildlife of the garden in question, this isn't necessarily so.

Ground elder is not native. It was introduced in the Middle Ages on account of its wide-ranging medicinal virtues. Creamy-white flowers rise above a forest of deep-green leaflets about 30cm high. They are not dissimilar to small versions of cow parsley or, indeed, elder itself, being slightly domed platters of tiny massed white blooms which display anytime a month either side of midsummer.

Most sites which have seen human habitation at some time are sure to have ground elder growing in the vicinity. Taken as a tea, the leaves and roots have both sedative and kidney-restorative properties. Applied as a warm, damp dressing to affected areas, ground elder provides real relief from swollen joint pain, rheumatism and gouty afflictions - so much so that an alternative name is 'goutweed'.

To do the job of clearing the ground in a nature-friendly manner you only need to rely on a border fork, hand fork and (most importantly) knee pads. Now is an ideal time to undertake this task, when the soil is fairly dry (preferably not caked) and before the goutweed comes into flower. The border fork (half as big as a digging fork, to get in amongst established ornamentals) is used to ease up the top 10cm or so of soil with repeated stabs and twists which loosens it. This action exposes some of the rubbery, yellow-brown tangled mat of offending roots. The hand fork then delves a little deeper, grubs them out and shakes a lot of the soil free, whereupon great wads can be lifted up and put aside for burning later. Surface roots are white and brittle, so need to be carefully hand-picked lest they break up and produce more plants in the future.

It is a big job and time-consuming. Even done with the utmost care and attention, ground elder is sure to return. But each successive sprouting will be weaker, there will be less of it, and consistently teasing it out of the soil whenever it is seen will eventually beat it into submission.

Slow and laborious though it may be, such a task is immensely satisfying through both its repeated actions and the unfolding results which are so visually obvious. If this really is all too much of a chore, another option is to love goutweed for the useful and wholesome, vitamin-packed food-source that it is and eat your fill. It cultivates itself and is freely available all summer long. Cooked exactly like spinach, the leaves provide delicious greens which are pleasantly aromatic.

Weeding so need not be a chore or boring. I am apt to become quite literally 'away with the fairies' whilst labouring quietly, lost in meditation and communion with the soil. A keen-eyed blackbird never fails to enhance the gardening experience. It sings with consummate ease and wistful beauty from the shrubbery, grabs wriggling worms and other tidbits with darting forays into the bare earth border or sits, beak blissfully agape and wings held out on the mossy grass above an ants' nest as the little insects swarm over the bird's body and amongst feathers, clearing it of mites and other irritations.

Hummingbird Hawk Moth

A hummingbird hawk moth provided some fascinating entertainment mid-week as Mrs Nails and I enjoyed a peaceful late meal in the garden. The amazing, chunky-bodied insect worked amongst a spray of red campion, that familiar hedgerow flower that is easy to grow, self-seeds freely and is more than happy to provide a lovely spray of deep pink, scattered blooms in a bed which is shady until the evening.

Hummingbird hawk moths fly during daylight hours. Their low, humming purr can often be heard before they are seen, wings a-blur, suspended in the air within tongue-dipping distance of the pretty, penny-sized decorated flasks of sweet nectar. The grey, chestnut and white moth darted from flower to flower, vanishing from time to time and then re-appearing just as suddenly. Having done the rounds in this little corner of the garden, with an hour and a half until sundown and honeysuckle against the fence coming into its own scent-wise, the busy entertainer was there one second and gone the next.

JUNE WEEK 3
JOBS TO DO THIS WEEK

IN THE GREENHOUSE

- Check all crops for pests and diseases.
- Ventilate freely.
- Water daily.
- Liquid feed established crops once.

ON THE PLOT

- Hoe amongst sweetcorn and dill (planted as companions).
- Water red cabbages.
- Last chance to plant out Brussels sprout seedlings.
- Water beans and peas, also any crops in pots.
- Water globe artichokes generously.
- Check asparagus for beetles/eggs and remove/destroy any found.
- Commence digging First Early potatoes.

JUNE Week 3: KOHL RABI

   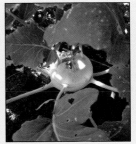

1. Kohl rabi is also known as 'turnip-rooted cabbage'. This quick-growing member of the brassica family starts off as pin-head sized, round, dark brown or black seeds.

2. Prepare a seedbed by removing all weeds and raking to a fine and even tilth. Mark out rows with string tied between two sticks. Sow seeds thinly into drills 1.5cm deep. Space rows 30cm apart.

3. As seedlings grow and develop leaves, gradually remove the poorest and weakest specimens to allow 15cm between plants. These are 'Purple Vienna' kohl rabi seedlings at nearly four weeks old and needing further thinning to fatten up.

4. A golf-ball sized 'Delikatess' kohl rabi ready for harvesting. Discard the leaves and shoots. Delicious steamed, sauteed or eaten raw either grated or cut into slices.

June

Asparagus Beetles

Asparagus beetles can do a lot of harm amongst the feathery plumes of this much sought-after vegetable delicacy. If left unchecked they are capable of severely weakening the long-term strength of the crop, thus reducing productivity. Controlling these pests is an important part of asparagus husbandry and a job which is wisely undertaken on an almost daily basis at this time of year.

The adults are colourful fellows, less than 1cm long, with distinctive, vibrant markings. Immediately below the small, black, two-antennae'd head is a block of orange (the 'thorax', or mid-part of an insect's body). This colouration extends along the side of the wing cases to circle around the rear end. The wing case tops (essentially, the beetle's back) have one black central stripe with a pattern of six creamy-white chequers. Underneath they are all black.

Asparagus beetles reside amongst the scales of emerging spears early in the season and nowadays will be found clambering amongst the greenery tops. As a defensive strategy they drop to the ground at the slightest disturbance. Cup a hand below individuals and give the branch a little jog to dislodge and catch the falling beetles, whereupon they can be dispatched with a sharp pinch.

Grubs (immature beetles) are much in evidence right now. They hatch in alarming numbers from dark, pinhead-sized, cylinder-shaped eggs which are attached to the dainty flowers and stalks either singly or in lines of maybe four or five. They are dull, brown-grey maggots with a shiny black head which sit amongst the lacy tracery of fine leaves, munching and growing quietly. They may be kept in check by carefully looking the plants over and squashing using thumb and first finger.

JUNE Week 4: WEEDS (2)

1. Pests and diseases can often be harboured on weeds. Fungal rust (above left), an orangey powder that coats leaves, can affect garlic, leeks and broad beans. It also thrives on groundsel (above right).

2. Aphids (above left, on poppy) are the great enemies of veggies like beans and artichokes. Fat hen, nasturtiums and dock (shown above right, as a seedling) frequently host vast armies of aphids which can then land on crops.

Asparagus beetles are potentially problematic all through the summer until the tops are cut and burnt (when all the goodness has been re-absorbed, in late autumn). Symptoms to look for, apart from the culprits themselves, are patches of browning, skeletal stems and branches. This die-back occurs when bark on the lower stems has been gnawed right around and is caused by both adults and juveniles.

When harvesting the crop ceases in June and asparagus is allowed to grow away, the flowers become extremely attractive to bees. Dozens of these essential pollinators flock to the bed during daylight hours, dodging in and out of the developing jungle, filling little sacks on their legs (actually modified hairs) with bright orange pollen.

In terms of securing a decent harvest, doing everything possible to attract bees (without whom arguably there would be no crops at all) is as important as being determined to keep asparagus beetle numbers in check. To this end, hand control is the only option available to wildlife-friendly growers. The chemical spray alternatives of pyrethrin or bifenthrin do not select the insects they kill and hence are not even on the agenda.

JOBS TO DO THIS WEEK

IN THE GREENHOUSE
- Ventilate freely.
- Water daily.
- Liquid feed established crops once.

ON THE PLOT
- Remove and compost rows of spent peas. Cut the stems (haulm) but leave roots in the soil to rot down naturally and slow-release their locked-up supplies of nitrogen.
- Tend outdoor tomatoes (tie in, pinch out).
- Check asparagus for beetles.
- Tend to runner beans.
- Re-sow climbing French beans where trashed by rabbits.
- Thin out Chevalier calibrese to 20cm spacings. Firm and water.
- Mow grass paths.
- Hand weed amongst swedes and squashes.
- Mourn the loss of carrots to badgers and resolve to grow this sweet root crop in containers out of harms way from now on!
- Water as needed.
- Summer prune top fruit.
- Spur prune step-over apples.
- Drench crops in pots.
- Sprinkle a top dressing of wood ash amongst tomatoes and hoe into the soil.
- Mark out rows for leeks.
- Control asparagus beetles.
- Plant out leeks into their final resting places.
- Plant out lettuce seedlings from friends.
- Hand weed and hoe a bit every day.
- Puddle in newly planted leeks daily.

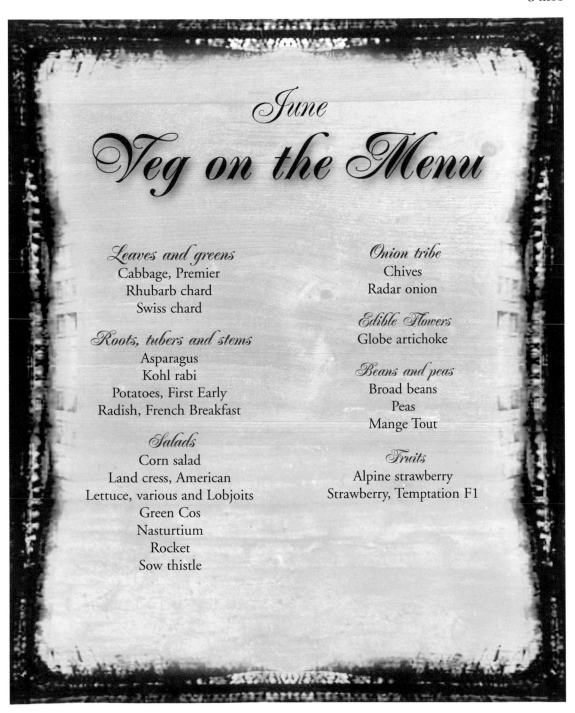

June

Veg on the Menu

Leaves and greens
Cabbage, Premier
Rhubarb chard
Swiss chard

Roots, tubers and stems
Asparagus
Kohl rabi
Potatoes, First Early
Radish, French Breakfast

Salads
Corn salad
Land cress, American
Lettuce, various and Lobjoits
Green Cos
Nasturtium
Rocket
Sow thistle

Onion tribe
Chives
Radar onion

Edible flowers
Globe artichoke

Beans and peas
Broad beans
Peas
Mange Tout

Fruits
Alpine strawberry
Strawberry, Temptation F1

July

Mullein Moth

At the peak of the season the caterpillars of Mullein moths can often be found amongst the leaves of cultivated ornamental Verbascums. They munch large holes and then reduce the plants to tattered skeletons. The peppered appearance of the caterpillars is quite distinctive. Each fleshy segment of aqua-blue is decorated with a ring of yellow which, in turn, is punctuated by pairs of black spots.

The leaf-eating habits of these creatures make them potential pests. They can be found throughout summer from late May, ranging from cute fellows less than 1.5cm to distinctly elephantine, well-fed monsters quadruple that size.

Early hatchings will be magically transforming into pupa this month. In this state they reside in the soil over-winter, rearranging their entire bodies by some miracle of nature before emerging as little reddish-brown moths next year. At no more than 2.5cm long, the winged insect at rest resembles a piece of plant stalk.

Control by hand-picking is the obvious solution but I have always had a soft-spot for both these moths and their favourite food plant, the great mullein (or 'Aaron's rod'), *Verbascum thapsus*. Here follows my technique for keeping the damage they do in Mrs Nails' flower beds to a minimum. It is, I think you'll find, both relaxing and effective.

Numerous Aaron's rod (free-seeding wild flowers) are encouraged to grow strategically amongst the veggies. Batches of the munching grubs are simply gathered up, when they are seen, from more highly-bred, prized specimens of cultivated Verbascums in the borders and relocated to the alternative (and preferred) food source. There they can be left eating away to their hearts' content.

Aaron's Rod

Great mullein seedlings are readily distinguishable on account of the low-growing rosette of grey-green, finely-furred leaves that develop in more unkempt corners of the veg patch. They are spared the hoe and allowed to grow. As biennials, great mullein will develop a strong, pad-like head of leaves this year and flower magnificently the next.

They transplant readily if treated with care whilst doing so, which means keeping plenty of soil around the roots and watering daily until they've recovered from the shock. In this way, you can move rogue mulleins to sites where they may prosper and bloom. A row planted with 30cm between them can look quite spectacular at the back of the veg plot in their second year. Thick wands rise to maybe 120 to 150cm, heavy with concealed pale-green buds which burst open from the bottom upwards from June to reveal eye-catching yellow flowers along the length. This display will continue on through to early autumn and be enjoyed by many garden allies such as bees and hoverflies.

Having passed their best and finished flowering the brown, crispy rods can be shaken into a paper bag and thousands of tiny seeds collected. These, sprinkled onto an undisturbed bit of sunny ground and lightly raked in, will ensure future supplies of flowers and moths. I love watching the progress of both, greeting each succeeding generation of plant and insect like old friends returning.

JULY Week 1: CABBAGE WHITE BUTTERFLIES

1. The large white butterfly lays tiny yellow eggs in clusters on brassicas like cabbages, kale, purple sprouting, Brussels sprouts and swedes. They are easy to detect on the underside of leaves.

2. Immediately upon hatching, caterpillars eat their egg cases then start tucking in to the foliage. Initially feeding together, yellow and black caterpillars grow quickly and spread out onto the whole plant.

3. When ready for the 'big change' fat caterpillars sneak away to find a handy crevice or woody cabbage stalk to pupate. An incredible transformation occurs inside the chrysalis. They completely rearrange their bodies, emerging as a butterfly to wreak more havoc on the plot.

4. Large white butterflies are beautiful but infuriating. Control can be achieved by rubbing out eggs with a thumb during regular searches. Caterpillars may be collected and relocated to nasturtiums grown as a 'sacrificial crop' elsewhere.

JOBS TO DO THIS WEEK

IN THE GREENHOUSE
- Ventilate freely.
- Water daily.
- Liquid feed once.
- Keep an eye out for pests and diseases.

ON THE PLOT
- Liquid feed outdoor tomatoes.
- Control asparagus beetles by hand picking.
- Puddle in leeks.
- Tidy up messy areas.
- Sort and store bags of manure and compost for future use.
- Plant carrots in pots and containers, Amsterdam Forcing, Berlicum and Autumn King.
- Harvest shallots and elephant garlic.
- Water beans, cucurbits, asparagus.
- Cut vegetation from around compost and leafmould heaps.
- Trim edges.
- Mow grass paths.
- Give a bucket of water to each young fruit tree in a dry spell.
- Suppress weeds around Victoria plum tree.
- Lay out garlic, shallots and elephant garlic on slatted pallets or chicken wire to dry in a sunny place.
- Hand weed asparagus bed.
- Tie in Ailsa Craig tomatoes.
- Keep the hoe busy even if you can't see the weeds.
- Tie in tomatillo plants to supporting canes.
- Clear spent broad beans to the compost heap.
- Keep harvesting First Early potatoes.

July

WEEK 2

Last of the Spring Peas

Spring-sown peas are just coming to an end and for visitors to the plot they have been a glorious delight. I only grow enough to consume fresh, being a firm advocate of eating produce mainly in season. However, if sufficient garden space and freezer room can be afforded, rest assured that peas raised in the kitchen garden or allotment are superb from frozen at any time of year.

A bumper crop has been harvested regularly since the end of May. Feltham First (a First Early variety), provided for the table initially, succeeded by generous pickings of Greenshaft (an Early Maincrop). These have been of the most wonderful size, taste and texture, the Greenshaft in particular being jam-packed with luscious peas. I don't think it's an exaggeration to consider that well-grown peas should be treated as delicacies of the highest order, either shelled and taken raw 'on the hoof' or removed to the kitchen for use in cooked dishes.

Cultivation techniques include meticulous and thorough ground preparations. A base-dressing of well rotted manure provides slow-release enrichment. This, allied with regular, consistent and appropriate husbandry through seed-sowing to flowering and fruition, including as much water as can be spared, may seem like a bit of a chore at times but this year at least it has been worth every effort (including re-sowing after slugs and snails had laid waste to rows of these veggies in a wet spring).

Peas are a perfect example of the real difference between the quality of home-grown produce and some of the stuff that is passed on to customers by the supermarkets. From the garden, their sweet loveliness is totally incomparable with the (admittedly nice but) bland nothingness of their mass-produced, chemically-enhanced, factory-farmed, pre-packed cousins. Firm pods, cracked open at the flower end and split straight down the middle with a thumbnail, can be eased apart to reveal lines of tightly fitting, shiny spheres of small-but-perfectly-formed peas. They deserve to be savoured when eaten, consumed with care and appreciation.

A rather more-ish summer dish which Mrs Nails likes to throw together on account of its ease of preparation and popularity with family and friends is her special Potato and Pea Salad.

Mrs Nails' Potato and Pea Salad

INGREDIENTS

Enough spuds to feed four
As many peas as you can spare or fancy
3 or 4 spring onions
Leaves from 3 sprigs of mint
Generous handful of chives
4 or 5 sprigs of parsley
Small bunch of coriander (optional)
Splosh of olive oil
Splash of balsamic vinegar
Juice from 1 lemon
Twist 'n' shake of salt and pepper to taste

METHOD

1. Cook the spuds until tender but firm, drain and leave to cool.
2. Dunk peas into boiling water, simmer for 2 minutes maximum, drain and leave to cool.
3. Prepare spring onions and herbs by chopping finely.
4. Toss all ingredients in a large bowl and mix well.

Mrs Nails' top tip: make absolutely sure that the spuds and peas are properly cooled, otherwise the mint will go black.

JULY Week 2: ONIONS AND ARTICHOKES

1. Onion sets planted at 15cm intervals in rows 30cm apart during March thrive when kept weed-free via regular hoeing. Edible portions should be swelling handsomely by high-summer. Annihilating weeds reduces competition for space, water, nutrients and light.

2. 'Bolted' onions that push up flower heads on thick stalks won't be any good for winter storage. They may be pulled up now, as and when required, for cooking or to liven up summer salads.

3. Fist-sized globe artichoke buds can be cut and boiled until tender. There is a mouthful of flesh to be scraped from the bottom of each bract and a gorgeous heart within to be savoured. The hairy 'choke' is aptly named and must be discarded.

4. Globe artichokes are thistles. Once the bud has burst into bloom it is no good for human consumption. Decorative flowers should be left to attract bees and other pollinating insects.

JOBS TO DO THIS WEEK

IN THE GREENHOUSE

- Ventilate freely.
- Water daily.
- Check for pests and diseases.
- Liquid feed tomatoes, peppers and aubergines.

ON THE PLOT

- Sow green manure Phacelia where broad beans were harvested.
- Hand weed amongst roots and Florence fennel.
- Hand weed ground cleared of shallots last week.
- Erect sturdy wire fence around sweetcorn to keep the badgers out (good luck!).
- Sow Swiss chard and leaf beet.
- Collect punnets of gooseberries to give to friends.
- Water newly-sown carrots in containers.
- Take down lines of exhausted peas.
- Train Marketmore cucumbers up supporting frame.
- Harvest the last of the garlic and set out to dry.
- Cut off top third of Jerusalem artichoke tops to lessen risk of wind damage in summer storms.
- Plant Hesta bush beans.
- Spot weed amongst the sprawling cucurbits.
- Puddle in leeks.
- Water all crops thoroughly if weather remains dry.
- Cut back plot edges.
- Harvest soft fruits.
- Drench strawberries in containers.
- Liquid feed cucumbers.
- Tie fan-trained fig tree to supporting framework of canes.
- Potter here and there.
- Get up early as often as possible to enjoy the dawn of each new day.
- Keep the hoe busy.
- Mulch all brassicas thickly with well-rotted manure.

July

Tending Asparagus

This week I've been providing support for the feathery tops of asparagus and suggest that you do the same. It is an important job to do in the summer when the plumes are tall and well grown. In this state they can act like big sails in windy or blustery wet weather and are liable to rock and sway in such conditions. This potentially has the effect of causing damage low down where stalks emerge from the ground. Such damage not only weakens the plant but can also lead to infection or rotting. Given the effort required for successful asparagus cultivation and long-term nature of the crop (many years if well tended), everything should be done to avoid this.

When the air is still, temperatures high and the veg plot provides a peaceful oasis in an otherwise crazy world, inclement conditions can seem far, far away. However, the occurrence of destructive summer storms towards the end of July is a near certainty and wise home producers take precautions before the weather breaks. To this end, secure two lengths of string taut between permanently positioned stout wooden posts which are driven into the ground at the end of each row. The asparagus is sandwiched between these strings. One pair is tied low down to hold the stems at the bottom and another pair higher up to steady the tops. Movement is further reduced by clasping them together at 'pinch points' with short lengths of knotted string. The job is completed by pushing canes in firmly at an angle (so as not to spear the mat of underground roots) and lashing the double strings to these for really storm-proof supports.

Butterflies

At last! Flushes of small tortoiseshell caterpillars have appeared in the last few days on the bank of stinging nettles which are allowed to grow unkempt at the bottom of the plot. Emerging from silken tents bound around the nettle tips, the yellow and black tiddlers feed and rest almost motionless. They give a unified, synchronised flick when disturbed, designed to alarm would-be predators.

The caterpillars grow rapidly and the leaves beneath become peppered with black specks of faeces. They more than double in size to where the oldest ones are this week, half an inch (1.5cm) long, black, with a double row of golden dashes along their backs and a single line either side. They are far more active at this stage, a writhing mass of leaf-munching eating machines. At about four weeks they will be up to 4cm in length and dispersed amongst the nettle bed. It is in here, suspended amongst the dried stems or other sheltered places in the vicinity, that each surviving caterpillar becomes a chrysalis. Metamorphosis (the process of transforming from juvenile to adult) is complete 12 or so days later, when they emerge as butterflies and take to the wing.

Small tortoiseshells have orange, dark-brown and yellow wings, with eye-catching bluey half-moons on the borders. They are commonly observed on buddleia which is blooming in riotous profusion right now. These will be the second brood of the year and show no interest in reproduction at this stage. Instead, they are the individuals that will hibernate, over wintering from late September/October in sheds, outbuildings, and under loose tree bark, in expectation of the following spring to come.

Birds

I watched a song thrush performing a useful service in the garden this week. The pretty, speckle-breasted fellow dropped down onto the lawn and, after checking the lie of the land, bounded into the flower border. After a bit of rummaging around, the bird reappeared with a meaty slug in its beak. Slugs are famously slimy, surrounding their bodies with a sticky goo which gardeners have to wipe off their fingers with a rag after handling because soap and water alone won't remove it.

I was curious to see how the thrush dealt with such an awkward customer. The answer was soon revealed as one slug, then another, was extracted from amongst the flowers and wiped quite carefully on the dry stone path which runs adjacent. These repeated, deliberate actions apparently scraped off the obnoxious coating. Thrush gathered up the naked slugs and flew off to enjoy a hearty meal.

JULY Week 3: LEAF BEET

1. Leaf beet is also called 'perpetual spinach'. An easy and reliable performer in the veg garden, it provides lovely big leaves in profusion. For generous portions of greens next spring, plant seeds now.

2. Leaf beet seeds are small and knobbly, but large enough to handle individually. Prepare a sunny bed by removing all weeds and raking to a fine tilth. Sow 1.5cm deep in rows 30cm apart.

3. 'Thinning' involves removing the weakest specimens to give the chosen few room to grow. As they develop, gradually pull out the poorest examples to eventually allow about 20cm between plants.

4. Rainbow chard is closely related to leaf beet. Luscious leaves are delicious when lightly steamed. Colourful stalks take a little longer, but provide an attractive dish when served with a knob of margarine and seasoning.

JULY WEEK 3

JOBS TO DO THIS WEEK

IN THE GREENHOUSE

- Ventilate freely.
- Water daily.
- Liquid feed all crops.
- Remove excess foliage from tomatoes.
- Inspect for pests and diseases.

ON THE PLOT

- Give Brussels sprouts a good drenching.
- Liquid feed all container grown tomatoes and strawberries.
- Water carrots in pots.
- Remove oldest and lowest leaves from Red Alert tomatoes.
- Tie in outdoor tomatoes to supports.
- Cut back plot edges here and there.
- Hoe amongst onions and elsewhere as and when time permits.
- Gather dried garlic and shallots in bunches and tie together for hanging in a dry and airy place.
- If rain is not forthcoming give water to beans and cucurbits especially.
- Thin container-grown carrots.
- Check over asparagus for beetles.
- Hand weed in the asparagus bed.
- Harvest the last First Early spuds, rake the patch level and sow crimson clover as green manure.
- Weed amongst the Second Early and Maincrop potatoes.

July

WEEK 4

Thoughts on Water Use

I've been following with interest tales from around the country of gardeners who are finding ingenious ways of getting around hose pipe restrictions and applaud those who have continued to nurture their patches in spite of the current climate. This is not to condone wasteful and unnecessary water use, but more to support what is essentially a beneficial activity, especially when conducted with sensitivity and respect for the wider environment and its inhabitants. I have always been minded to resist any such ban should it be enforced in this neck of the woods and then argue the case in a legal arena should it come to that. My position remains unchanged.

For many of us, growing vegetables is more than just a pastime: it is a way of producing food which is sustainable. We are in control of how the land is treated and what goes into it. Growing your own allows for food decisions to be made based on ethical, social and political concerns. Home-grown veggies demand no air miles or environmentally heavy-handed procedures to get from plot to plate. Preparation amounts to little more than gathering, which means some strenuous fork-work at worst (spuds) or mellow picking at best (runner beans) and frequently scrubbing with a brush and bucket of water. No machinery, factories or wasteful packaging.

Everything in the shops has guzzled water from the off. Vast quantities are used to irrigate crops, often in places abroad where there is none available for the local people to use in their day-to-day living. Harvesting and preparing is heavily reliant on industry to manufacture metals, plastics, wood products and fuels. In short, veg on the shop shelves has arguably accounted for infinitely more water use than anything grown in the kitchen garden or down the allotment. These reasons alone are enough for me to be able to comfortably justify continued responsible watering of the garden even before considering further hideous wastage by water companies (via leaking pipes), and industrial processes (consider the quantities of H_2O needed to manufacture a single daily newspaper, for example, or the fact that one pint of beer consumes well in excess of one pint of water before you drink it).

Pleasure gardening of ornamentals has benefits, too, which are real in terms of the health and well-being of those who participate in creating or enjoying their resulting tranquil havens. Does this relaxation of mind and body influence water consumption? Observing how a spell amongst her flowers relieves Mrs Nails of her work stresses at the end of a long day, I am inclined to think it does.

JULY Week 4: SUMMER CROPS

1. Beetroot crop thick and fast in high summer. In the kitchen, twist leaves off about 5cm up the stalks rather than cutting. This prevents all the lovely beetroot-red juice from bleeding away whilst simmering to tenderness in the pot.

2. Courgettes should be producing prolifically. As with beans, the more you pick the more they deliver. Slice thinly, flash-fry in olive oil and season with salt 'n' pepper for a delicious snack at any time of the day.

3. Climbing French and runner beans begin to produce in abundance about now. Pick daily before they become tough and stringy. Top, tail, slice and steam for sumptuous portions of summer fare.

4. Florence fennel bulbs are fat and handsome. A spray of feathery green leaves fans out like a strutting peacock's tail. These can flavour soups and stews. The liquorice-tasting bulbs are wonderful when sliced and diced in salads or slow-roasted in the oven.

Late Carrots

Rock-hard ground at this time of year is not good news for badgers. Their favourite food, earthworms, are hiding far down below and scratching around for a meal is hard work. Gardens are very attractive to badgers right now, especially when stocked with tempting foods and moist soils. Their damaging night-time exuberances in the veg plot are often at their worst in high-summer, with carrots top of the list of delicacies. This exceptionally hot, dry summer is no exception and despite my best efforts I am in a race to see who can eat the remaining standing crop first!

To offset losses to badgers a sowing of carrots made now, in deep containers, will provide sweet roots for use throughout the winter months. Kinbi F1 is a superbly flavoured golden-yellow carrot which grows fast and Nantes 2 is a tasty variety which performs well late in the

JULY WEEK 4

JOBS TO DO THIS WEEK

IN THE GREENHOUSE

- Water all crops daily.
- Ventilate freely.
- Liquid feed once or twice this week.
- Keep a keen eye out for pests and diseases.

ON THE PLOT

- Water carrots in containers.
- Collect manure from outside sources in plastic bags and deliver to the plot for future use.
- Drench the roots of chard and leaf beet.
- Water tomatoes and strawberries in containers.
- Admire the first Giant Single sunflower bloom of the season, if you're lucky.
- Keep a zero tolerance policy towards weeds in the asparagus bed during regular checks for beetles and their grubs.
- De-leaf to the lowest truss of tomatoes on the Ailsa Craig variety.
- Plant out any spare lettuce seedlings gifted from neighbours.
- Mow grass paths.
- Water root zone of veggies that look like they need it.
- Keep the hoe busy.
- Potter and mooch productively in the evenings.
- Prune Oullins Gage plum.

season too. Use the deepest pots available. Council recycling bins are perfect. After filling them almost to the top with a light, peat-free multi-purpose compost, seeds are scattered evenly over the surface, raked-in and smoothed-over using the fingertips.

Daily watering with a rose-ended can will work in tandem with plenty of sunshine and warm temperatures to ensure swift germination and speedy growth. Thinning out is important after a fortnight or so but, when sown thinly and raised in this way, you need be less concerned with overcrowding because the roots should jostle for space and plunge into the depths. The containers can be kept out of the reach of marauding Billies and ringed with Vaseline to deter molluscs (slugs and snails). When the weather turns cold come November time, the whole lot can go into the greenhouse to keep fresh and ready for use.

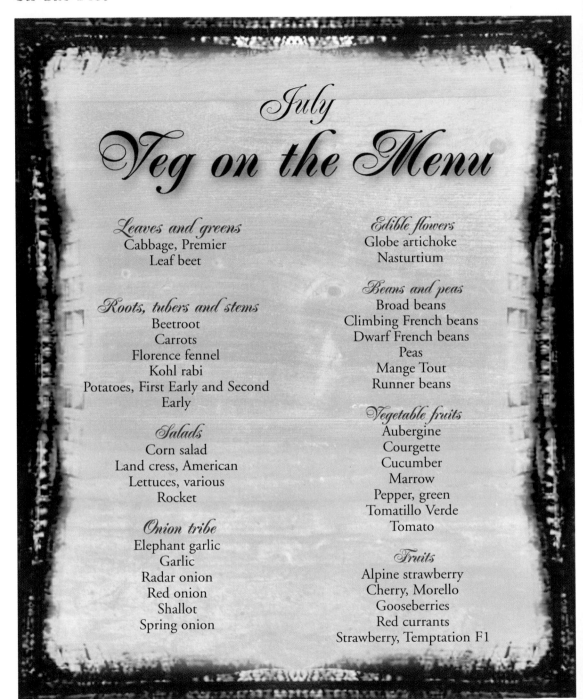

July
Veg on the Menu

Leaves and greens
Cabbage, Premier
Leaf beet

Roots, tubers and stems
Beetroot
Carrots
Florence fennel
Kohl rabi
Potatoes, First Early and Second
Early

Salads
Corn salad
Land cress, American
Lettuces, various
Rocket

Onion tribe
Elephant garlic
Garlic
Radar onion
Red onion
Shallot
Spring onion

Edible flowers
Globe artichoke
Nasturtium

Beans and peas
Broad beans
Climbing French beans
Dwarf French beans
Peas
Mange Tout
Runner beans

Vegetable fruits
Aubergine
Courgette
Cucumber
Marrow
Pepper, green
Tomatillo Verde
Tomato

Fruits
Alpine strawberry
Cherry, Morello
Gooseberries
Red currants
Strawberry, Temptation F1

August

WEEK 1

Harvesting French Beans

I was pleased to be able to gather a harvest from the slow-to-get-going climbing French beans this week. All being well, you should be able to do the same.

As seeds, the Blue Lake variety were sown in pots in the greenhouse during April then planted outside around mid-May. Another batch was put direct into the soil at the end of May/beginning of June. They all struggled initially due to the nibbling attentions of a small army of rabbits who take in the bottom of the veg patch as part of their rounds. The twitch-nose little rascals got into the habit of grazing off the tender shoots of my climbers (and tasty tips of leeks!).

Until about a month ago the framework of canes erected for them to twine around and clamber up was looking decidedly bare. However, a few days of consistent, concentrated manual watering and lovely hot sunshine proved to be perfect ingredients for the beans. They put on a spurt of growth which was too much even for hungry bunnies, shooting up and away. The result now is that the pot-sown beauties are lolling over the tops of their supports, plastered with creamy flowers and sporting abundant dangling bunches of pale green, cylindrical beans. The second (direct) sowing is playing catch up and

should, all being well, provide an ample bounty to extend the cropping season well into autumn.

Direct sown in June, dwarf French beans Aiguillon have been in full production for a couple or three weeks now. It's great fun to seek out the long, slender, pencil-podded beans in amongst the lush, bushy, low-growing foliage. I'm particularly partial to dwarf French beans served with a minimum of fuss. Large portions are simply topped 'n' tailed then steamed and enjoyed as a side dish, complete with light dusting of seasoning and a drizzle of olive oil.

Beans want to reproduce and going to seed is how they do it. Once the pods are fat, flowering ceases because the job is done. To ensure a continuous supply of food, take care to pick regularly and harvest every bean except the very smallest ones. This includes any big, tough customers that have been previously overlooked and allowed to develop too much. These don't make for the best eating but are usefully consigned to the compost heap for recycling. In this way, the hard-working plants are kept youthful by constantly stimulating them into bearing fresh flushes of flowers and resulting tasty fare.

AUGUST Week 1: SOWING SPRING ONIONS

1. Prepare a seedbed for spring onions by raking soil to a fine and crumbly tilth. If planning to cultivate more than one row allow 10cm between lines marked with string tied tight between two canes.

2. Sow the pinhead-sized black seeds 1cm deep, carefully and evenly. Emptying seeds into the palm of one hand and sowing with thumb and forefinger of the other is the easiest way.

3. Spring onion seedlings come up like blades of grass. Provided they are not sown too thickly there is no need to thin them out.

4. Harvesting is simple. Gently pull a handful from loosened soil. Dunk in water to clean mud off the roots prior to eating in salads and stir-fries from October onwards.

Coping with Horseflies

Horseflies can be an unpleasant menace in the garden anytime during the summer, at times reaching alarming numbers. One of these insects landed on me this week. With jaws like tiny side-on pliers it sunk vicious mouth-parts into the thin skin on the back of my hand in an attack so stealthy, silent and painful that, despite the heat, I was forced to roll down my sleeves, tuck in and button up my shirt. After that, even the slightest hint of anything landing about my person caused a nervously violent twitch!

Shortly after, whilst taking a break from gardening, I watched another of these creatures through a hand lens. It landed on my trousers and was vainly trying to get a hold of the thick material. When observed close up, this horsefly was amazing to look at, decorated with quite

AUGUST WEEK 1
JOBS TO DO THIS WEEK

IN THE GREENHOUSE

- Ventilate freely.
- Water crops daily.
- Check for pests and diseases.
- Liquid feed a couple of times this week.

ON THE PLOT

- Water thoroughly strawberries, tomatoes and carrots in containers.
- Collect and deliver manure. Store it to season for use in a few months' time.
- Cut blighted potato haulms and burn immediately to kill the fungus.
- De-leaf Ailsa Craig tomatoes.
- Tie Brussels sprouts plants to stout stakes to keep their roots firm.
- Mulch Brussels sprouts with well-rotted manure.
- Drench brassicas with strong nettle and comfrey solution to control caterpillars.
- Liquid feed all beans.
- Give every young fruit tree a bucket of water each.
- Hand pick caterpillars from brassicas.
- Check over outdoor tomato foliage for signs of blight. Pick off and remove anything that looks suspicious.
- Cut nettles around plot edges where they are interfering with day-to-day duties, and compost.
- Keep the hoe busy.

beautiful brown and black marbling on its lozenge-shaped body and translucent wings. Such a handsome beast would surely be more lauded if it were benign, but this possessor of a painful bite is largely unloved. Anyone who has been the subject of their unnerving attentions will appreciate why. The individual trying to access soft skin was merely brushed aside, not flattened, as the perfectness of its purpose coupled with handsome colourations and patterning deemed it a worthy survivor.

My swollen hand itched painfully for a few days but neat lavender oil rubbed onto the affected area kept it bearable. When horseflies are out and about, insect repellent applied to bare body parts and brim of hat is now standard. Citronella oil is good and a number of proprietary products will also do the trick.

August

Florence Fennel in August

Why not start harvesting Florence fennel when the sun is shining? The distinctive, flattened bulbs are uniquely flavoured and as big as a man's splayed hand. They stand proud of the soil, very pale green beneath a branching fan of delicate, darker, feathery top growth. This vegetable has an air of exotic decadence about it but is a fairly reliable cropper if seed is sown into a fertile soil and full sun during early April. Husbandry is straightforward enough, with 'bulb fennel' (as it is alternatively known) germinating readily, demanding little more than to be kept well watered and weed free.

I grow the Zefa Fino variety of Florence fennel at approximately 30cm intervals. Establishing rows of plants with enough space to swell requires thinning out surplus or weak seedlings in progressive stages from when they are large enough to handle. It can be difficult sacrificing perfectly good plants during these times but failure to thin out is a false economy as the resulting produce, albeit delicious, will be under-sized.

Such thinnings need not go to waste. They are lovely when finely chopped and taken raw, adding clean, invigorating, breath-freshening qualities to salads. Basking in a long line between swedes and parsnips (both coming along nicely, and staple winter fare) this season's batch looks particularly handsome.

Florence fennel has many uses in the kitchen. At this time of the year it is arguably at its best when the trimmed-up bulb is delivered with minimal fuss on a plate as a supper time centrepiece after a long, slow oven-roasting, whole, in the company of red onions.

Watering Fruit Trees

Recently planted young trees have three important needs in their initial couple or four years while they get well established and bedded in. One is a firm footing, which is achieved via the 'slot planting' method which I prefer when planting bare-rooted stock, from October until the end of February. This involves tucking the roots into a simple notch cut open vertically by inserting a spade into the ground, thus ensuring virtually no disturbance or upheaval to the surrounding soil.

Another is freedom from competition by grasses and flowers around the base. This is granted by use of a 'mulch mat'. Either cut from old carpet or purchased purpose made, a 90cm square piece will suppress immediate neighbouring growth. An alternative is to apply a similarly wide 5cm thick layer of bark chippings around, but not touching, the circumference of the tree.

The third vitally important need is water. It is probably true to say that most newly-establishing young trees fail to naturally receive enough to drink throughout their formative summers. Top fruit such as apples, pears and plums are a long-term investment, so put regular watering high up on the list of dry-season jobs to do. See that they get consistent supplies of essential liquid at least fortnightly either by pouring on two or three bucket loads or drenching with a hose for 15 minutes or so each. Weakened future specimens, or at worst dead trees, can be avoided by making sure that an adequate amount of the good stuff is given slowly so it can drain deep down to the roots.

AUGUST Week 2: FARMYARD MANURE

1. In 1950, as mechanisation kicked in after World War Two, there were still 300,000 horses working on farms. Nowadays a working horse is a novelty. Horse manure is possibly the best organic matter that growers can lay their hands on.

2. Even a dollop shovelled up off the road is worth its weight in gold to a gardener! Manure can be heavy and dirty to handle so watch your back while loading and unloading.

3. Well-rotted manure teems with life. Worms are central to keeping soils healthy as they tunnel, burrow and move nutrients from one place to another. Manure is bulky: it lightens heavy growing mediums and binds those which are light.

4. Manure is a slow-release fertiliser containing all the nutrients demanded for healthy vegetable growth. Flopping a handful or three around the base of cabbages or kale now will give them a really productive boost.

AUGUST WEEK 2

JOBS TO DO THIS WEEK

IN THE GREENHOUSE

- Ventilate freely.
- Water daily.
- Liquid feed all crops twice this week.
- Keep a watch for pests and diseases.

ON THE PLOT

- Water crops in containers.
- Water beans.
- Hoe amongst chard, leaf beet and other rows of handsome crops.
- Hand weed asparagus bed and around the celeriac.
- Clear encroaching vegetation from around compost bins and clean these out ready for delivery of manure.
- Hand weed ripening maincrop onions.
- Liquid feed cucumbers.
- Check Brussels sprouts for caterpillars and relocate to sacrificial bed of nasturtiums.
- Prune and tie in Morello cherry.
- Clear path by cobnuts and filberts so you can spy and admire the lovely nut clusters.
- Cut back plot edges.
- Tidy and wash pots which tend to litter the place.

August

WEEK 3

Field Beans as a Green Manure

'Green manures' can be used to invigorate and replenish soil in the vegetable patch. These plants are not grown for harvesting crops but to be either cut down or dug in to the plot so as to add nutrients and organic matter in order to feed and sustain the health of a gardener's most valuable asset – the soil.

Field beans are ideal for this purpose and during the salad days of mid-June, on previously continuously cultivated ground vacated by the lifting of autumn-sown Radar onions, I had planted a batch. Having thoroughly weeded the bed first, and after giving it a light forking, the 1.5cm dried brown seeds were broadcast sown (scattered as if feeding chickens) then raked in. In the following couple of months they grew like the clappers, to the point this week of being 45cm tall and laden with trusses of the palest, pinky-cream flower buds. Top growth, or 'haulm', is bulky, lush and thick.

At this stage, before they either get tough and woody or set seed, cut them down. All being well, field beans will respond to such treatment by producing a second flush of foliage which can, at the appropriate time, be chopped off again. The haulms are left where they fall and will be incorporated into the growing medium, as humus, by earthworms and other creatures.

Humus (decomposed vegetable matter) is important in soils. Where they are light and free draining (sandy, silty, or chalky) it improves moisture retaining qualities. In heavy (clay) soils it opens up the texture and makes them easier to work. Humus also increases fertility by adding a cocktail of nutrients.

Like all members of the pea family (legumes or Fabaceae), field beans are able to increase levels of nitrogen available to plants in a soil. This nutrient is a vital requirement for all leafy, green crops but is only sourced naturally in the atmosphere. In order to access nitrogen, plants rely on bacteria to refine it (through 'nitrification') into nitrates which they can consume. Legumes do this by forming small nodules on their roots. These nodules provide a protected environment for nitrogen-fixing bacteria to reside in. As a kind of payment for this safe haven the plants receive ample supplies of 'N'.

It is fine to leave the roots of field beans in the soil to slowly rot away over the winter months after cutting them off for a second time. Coupled with a mulch of well-rotted manure or humus, applied just before the onset of winter, they will act like a slow release fertiliser. This quality can be exploited by us gardeners when choosing where to nurture crops next season. As and when the harvest comes in over the next couple of months, I advise sowing more field beans in the gaps and managing them to keep your soil in the peak of condition.

AUGUST WEEK 3
JOBS TO DO THIS WEEK

IN THE GREENHOUSE
- Ventilate freely.
- Water all crops every other day.
- Be alert for pests and diseases.
- Sow cabbages: Offenham Compacta, Ormskirk Savoy.

ON THE PLOT
- Liquid feed calibrese.
- Water container carrots, tomatoes and strawberries.
- Sow Tiger lettuce and put seed tray in shade to germinate (lettuce seeds don't respond well in high summer temperatures).
- Water purple sprouting.
- Cut down field beans sown as green manure and dig into the soil.
- Water all beans, fruit trees, spinach, chard, beetroot and rhubarb.
- Tie dried garlic and elephant garlic into bunches for store.
- Keep busy with the hoe.
- Collect pot marigold seeds in dry weather for next year.
- Feel the magic of mid-August with a cup of tea or something stronger.

AUGUST Week 3: HARVESTING AND STORING ONIONS

1. Onions are ripe for harvesting when shiny bulbs lift easily from the ground and roots are withered and dry.

2. Lifted onions need sorting. Soft bulbs are no good and should go on the compost heap. Those showing brown at the neck or a thick central stem won't keep long. They are best eaten first.

3. All the others can be tied into bunches and hung in a sheltered, frost-free place until needed in the kitchen.

4. Alternatively, keep onions one-deep in plastic fruit trays. Stored this way after a good season, they should last well into early next summer.

August

WEEK 4

Season of 'Mists and Mellow Fruitfulness'

The nineteenth century poet John Keats immortalised these months after late summer when he famously described them as being 'the season of mists and mellow fruitfulness'. His inspiration was the rolling chalk hills and water meadows at Twyford Down, near Winchester. Although those words were penned a long time ago, and since then in places the world (including that pocket of Hampshire countryside) has altered beyond recognition, some things remain reassuringly constant.

Nowadays, Keats would need to shield his eyes and nostrils from an incessant roar and stench, courtesy of the stream of constantly moving vehicles pouring through the gashing cut of M3 extension in his beloved central southern England. However, elsewhere he could still stand in spirit if not person and thrill to the consistency of that never-ending cycle of change which punctuates the gardening year (and many other things besides).

It was present this week, that tangible magic, as Monday dawned with an unmistakeable autumnal nip in the air. An invigorating, shot-in-the-arm freshness to contrast with the long, lazy heat and humidity dished out in abundance by the passing summer. For me, it was enough to prompt the donning of a body-warmer which had been hung up in the porch over the last few months. Rummaging through the pockets was a journey back in time, to April and May, with fond memories jogged by the crumpled empty seed packets, plant labels, tangled lengths of string and other oddments re-discovered there.

Tiger Lettuce

In the greenhouse, rows of handsome aubergines are laden with glistening fruits emerging in super-slow motion like fantastic, elongated, purple eggs out of thick, ridged, spiny stems, borne from a flower pretty enough to be cultivated in its own right. Pots of chillies are massed with contorted pods which curl and bulge like arthritic fingers shining green and scarlet red. I've been preparing for next year by sowing lettuces. Tiger is an iceberg variety which can be sown from February until September and a planting now should, all being well, provide crisp heads for cutting early next season.

Prepare a seed tray by three-quarters filling with potting compost, then gently level with a flat wooden firming board. Tiger lettuce seeds are brown and shaped like tiny grains of rice. They are fiddly customers so use tweezers to handle them and insert 25mm deep at regular 5cm intervals. This allows for about 28 seedlings to develop per standard-sized tray.

Within ten days or so, when they have two leaves, carefully prick out into small individual pots with John Innes Number 1. This is an ideal medium for growing on seedlings. Subsequently they can go into larger receptacles containing a peat-free compost and be nurtured in an unheated greenhouse or cold frame (a well lit, frost-free, protected environment) for a late spring harvest. Tiger lettuce seeds will not germinate above 18 degrees centigrade so site your trays outside in the cool shade if temperatures are high at this crucial time.

AUGUST WEEK 4
JOBS TO DO THIS WEEK

IN THE GREENHOUSE

- Ventilate freely.
- Water every third day.
- Liquid feed once.

ON THE PLOT

- Start getting the shallots in store.
- Clear caterpillars from Chevalier calibrese and Brussels sprouts.
- Harvest maincrop onions.
- Check over all areas.
- Mulch January King cabbages with well-rotted manure.
- Tidy here and there.
- Pot on Tiger lettuce.
- Keep your hoe busy.

AUGUST Week 4: FLOWERS IN THE VEG PATCH

1. Traditional agricultural weeds like corn marigold (above), cornflower, corncockle and poppies grew in vast numbers before weedkiller use became widespread.

2. If given a chance they will thrive on regularly disturbed land and, like the cornflower above, are very much at home growing amongst vegetables.

3. Bees and other beneficial insects find the pretty blooms of weeds such as corncockle (shown) irresistible. A few specimens can be allowed to flower and set seed.

4. Wild flowers on the plot are pleasing to look at. Letting some grow, like this beautiful poppy, helps to create a healthy, naturally balanced environment.

August

WEEK 5

Cosmos for a Wedding

A wedding at its best is a wonderful celebratory party, shared by lovers in the company of family and friends. An occasion when the troubles and strife of past and future are put aside for a day of unashamed commitment and unity. The last day of August witnessed one such occasion. My sister-in-law and partner sealed their relationship of sixteen years with a beautifully intimate, home-spun civil ceremony at a rather picturesque location just a short drive from town. And the weather was perfect too, warm with sunny spells, distinctly English.

For Mrs Nails, ever the Older Sister, it was a time to rush and tear, organising this and setting up that with almost military precision, the moment of truth looming larger and closer on the horizon as summer ticked by and autumn beckoned. One of the most important things on her list of jobs to do for the Big Day was supply ample armfuls of flowers, for button-holes, posies and bouquets.

Cosmos is easy to grow (just follow the seed packet instructions) and was earmarked for this role months ago when Mrs Nails first pictured the scene in her head. During recent weeks, dead-heading after work has been a daily pleasure, undertaken with a cup of tea and cigarette. Then, on wedding day morning I was sent out into the garden with instructions to remove every bloom from three towering clumps which she had carefully nurtured from seed sown in March.

Cosmos flowers in profusion. The blooms are simple but showy, with a frill of petals arranged around a central yellow disc which contains the reproductive organs. Ranging from pure white through pale mauve to deep purple, they dance by the many-dozen amongst a billowing mass of feathery foliage. Constant tending should stimulate the production of numerous green, button-like buds and subsequent riots of colour well into October/November.

Domestication of ornamentals entails selecting features that please the human eye. Happily with cosmos, this is not at the expense of their wildlife value. Even whilst snipping lengths of stalk crowned with flowers, an array of amazingly striped hoverflies and fluffy bumble bees continued to buzz and dart in my midst, working the flowers even after they had been gathered in bunches laid out for tying on the lawn.

AUGUST WEEK 5
JOBS TO DO THIS WEEK

IN THE GREENHOUSE

- Ventilate.
- Water all crops once every three days.
- Pot on Offenhams Myatt cabbages.
- Prick out Offenhams Compacta cabbages.
- Prick out Ormskirk Savoy.
- Check for pests and diseases.

ON THE PLOT

- Keep the hoe busy around maturing and ripening crops.
- Thoroughly weed, turn, rake and firm a piece of ground in preparation for planting winter Radar onions.
- Remove tatty outer leaves on celeriac.
- Remove old leaves from parsnips which can provide hiding places for slugs and snails.
- Check over and hand weed amongst swedes.
- Harvest Red Baron onions.
- Keep harvesting beans.
- Have a fire to dispose of rubbish and stuff which is unsuitable for composting.
- Position flat stones (roofing slates are ideal) under squashes to lift them off the soil and assist ripening.
- Check brassicas for caterpillars and remove by hand. Relocate amongst nasturtiums grown especially.
- Remove husky skins from Maincrop onions and place in plastic fruit crates for storing.
- Pick cosmos and other beautiful flowers for bouquets and posies for the house and to give to friends.
- Remove perennial weeds such as bindweed and horsetail wherever they're appearing on the plot.
- Start Maincrop potato harvest.
- Remove dried skin and stems from red onions in preparation for store.
- Keep on top of the weeds.

AUGUST Week 5: TENDING PARSNIPS

1. Badgers have a sweet tooth and love to dig up young parsnips. The keen gardener can dissuade these handsome beasts from such vandalism by spraying human urine around the growing veggies.

2. Browned-off leaves serve no useful purpose apart from providing sheltered hidey-holes from slugs and snails. Keep the crop clean and pests at bay by removing them to the compost heap.

3. Weeds compete with vegetables for water, light and nutrients. Conserve these valuable resources for food plants by tickling between the rows with a hoe.

4. Enjoy out-of-season 'snips by lifting a bunch or three and placing in the refrigerator for a couple of days to replicate the sweetening effect which frost has on these edible roots.

August
Veg on the Menu

Leaves and greens
Calibrese
Chard
Leaf beet
Sow thistle

Roots, tubers and stems
Beetroot
Carrots
Florence fennel
Potatoes

Salads
Lettuce, various

Onion tribe
Garlic
Onion, Maincrop
Onion, Radar
Red onions
Shallots
Spring onion

Beans and peas
Climbing French bean
Dwarf French beans
Runner beans

Vegetable fruits
Aubergine
Courgette
Cucumber
Pepper, Green, Red and Chilli
Tomatillo
Tomato

Fruits
Apples, windfall Bramley from
next door
Apples, Scrumptious
Blackberry
Black currant
Raspberry

Cereal
Sweetcorn

September   WEEK **1**

Spiders for Natural Balance

Whilst looking at an orb web spider poised in the centre of a silken snare this week, spread-eagled and ready to spring into action, I was struck by the beauty of her appearance and creation. It was a Garden Cross, or Diadem. These familiar beige and tan spiders, so common in the garden and wider countryside at this time of the year, are striped like mini eight-legged tigers and dotted around the rough plot edges in their webs wherever vegetation gives height enough for them to secure an anchor.

The individual under close inspection, a particularly fine and plump specimen as big as a two-pence piece, was just one of dozens hawking their trade all over the place. She had slung her gossamer net between an untrimmed branch of *Lonicera nitida* (an evergreen, small-leaved honeysuckle commonly used for hedging), stinging nettle tip, plastic bucket and seed tray on top of a pile of unwashed pots.

Garden Cross spiders construct the most fabulous webs afresh every night and do a great service to gardeners in catching innumerable insect pests. This one sat quite motionless with no fewer than 45 threads radiating out in a fan and over 50 lines circling around like the ever-increasing rings on a cut-through section of tree trunk. Looking up from my seated position outside the greenhouse door, I could see that she was not alone. The entire section of hedge, unclipped throughout summer and now a jumbled riot of exploding *Lonicera*, privet, trailing barbed bramble shoots and lolling white trumpets of hedge bindweed, was alive with dozens of these pretty little spiders. Each was biding their time in the early morning sunshine.

All species of spider are welcome when a natural balance between predators and prey is encouraged as an alternative to chemical pesticides. They play a crucial role in maintaining the ecological harmony of a healthy garden. This is just one reason why I'm none too precious about neat and tidy hedges and edges, preferring to encourage wildlife by cutting once a year only (in late winter).

The unkempt (but productive) orchard is in stark contrast to the orderly neatness of my carefully tended veggie growing areas. Here, nothing will be cleared or tidied for a few months yet. Skeletal structures of hogweed, corncockle, mullien, knapweed, teasel, willowherb and various bird-seed descended cereals (amongst others) provide a naturally ebbing flow of cover amongst the fruit and nut trees. This space becomes increasingly important for feeding and over-wintering opportunities not just to spiders, but also frogs, slow worms and other garden mini-beasts as the adjacent veg patch is gradually cleared and crops are harvested.

On an autumnal morn, getting lassoed by gossamer on that initial trek up the garden path is slightly irritating (more so if you prefer your spiders at a distance) and tickly when the route is overhung with trees and shrubs. It is easy enough to avoid, however. Simply hold a twig in front of your face which breaks and removes any misplaced webs as you pass through. It's a neat trick which I learnt many years ago as a front-line conservationist working in the New Forest.

SEPTEMBER Week 1: LEAFMOULD AND COMPOST

1. Deciduous trees drop foliage in autumn and regrow it fresh each spring. Their leaves are of great value in the garden for maintaining and enhancing soil structure, moisture-retaining properties and encouraging abundant soil life.

2. Collected leaves can be piled up and left for a year. Keep them moist if summer is dry. The decomposing power of fungi break leaves down into rich, dark and crumbly 'leafmould'. In this state it can be applied to the soil surface as a mulch or incorporated via digging.

3. Any non-woody organic ingredients can be added to a compost heap. Avoid potatoes and tomatoes which can spread disease, invasive weeds, and cooked food waste which may attract vermin. Grass clippings are perfect unless recently given a weed and feed treatment.

4. The compost heap doesn't have to be fancy. Wooden pallets lashed together with wire are perfect. Just pile the refuse on top. There is no need to turn or tend unless feeling energetic or in a hurry. Natural processes will work their magic in twelve months or so.

SEPTEMBER WEEK 1
JOBS TO DO THIS WEEK

IN THE GREENHOUSE
- Ventilate.
- Water any seedlings daily.
- Water once every three days, once with nettle & comfrey added as a liquid feed.
- De-leaf lower foliage from tomatoes.
- Pot on Offenhams Compacta and Ormskirk Savoy cabbages.

ON THE PLOT
- Thin out Ailsa Craig tomato leaves to let in the light to ripen fruits.
- Hoe bed prepared for winter onions.
- Keep collecting manure from outside sources for future use.
- Clear all vegetation from spuds in the ground and burn.
- Cut down top third of asparagus ferns to lessen risk of wind rock.
- Sow green manures where ground would otherwise stand empty over winter.
- Check all brassicas for caterpillars and relocate to nasturtiums.
- Keep on hand weeding and hoeing whenever you can.
- Deadhead butterfly bushes to stimulate fresh flushes of flowers.
- Formatively prune peach for a fan.
- Mulch peach with newspaper, grass clippings and manure.
- Keep container carrots moist but not wet.
- Remove lower leaves of Brussels sprouts which are looking tatty and discoloured.
- Hand weed amongst cucumbers.
- Drench strawberries in pots.
- Potter and mooch.
- Stay busy with the hoe when the soil is dry.
- Hoe between standing crops of beans and celeriac amongst others.
- Remove dying rhubarb leaves to the compost heap.
- Hand weed asparagus bed.

September WEEK 2

Autumn Weeding

Conditions that hark back to those timeless, lazy, halcyon days of summer become fewer and further between as the year presses relentlessly on. However, settled spells of lovely calm dry weather are just one of the many delights which September serves up and provide vegetable gardeners with a perfect opportunity to get on top of the weeding. Their growth is currently slowing all the time and hitting weeds hard now will make essential winter maintenance of the plot much easier and more pleasurable.

Edible crops are generally selectively bred versions of plants which occur naturally in the wild, either in this country or abroad. For maximum culinary potential, competition from vigorous and highly fecund (rapidly reproducing) so-called weeds must be kept to a minimum. A Dutch hoe is the perfect tool for this job when used during fine weather at this time of year on weeds not far past the seedling stage. It makes keeping the patch clean and free from those that would otherwise vie with the veg for valuable soil moisture and nutrient reserves a cinch.

Work slowly and carefully, sliding the blade back and forth, tickling through the surface without digging into it. Weeds are sliced off from their roots. A generous dose of autumnal sunshine will quickly dry them to a crispy frazzle. Thus, the good earth is kept open and friable on top, allowing easy penetration of water when the rains come and preventing 'surface capping'. This can occur when fine particles which make up soils become dusty and/or compacted, bonding together to form a crust (often the result of trampling). Moisture then has a tendency to run off before having a chance to percolate down. Surface capping can also prevent emergent seedlings from breaking out into the light.

SEPTEMBER Week 2: PLANTING WINTER ONIONS

1. Now is the time to plant winter onion sets, sometimes called 'autumn onions'. They can tough out even the harshest winter, swell up in spring and ripen for an early harvest in late-May.

2. Onions like a sunny position and firm root-run. Lightly fork over the selected plot and sprinkle wood ash thinly but evenly. Rake the bed to a fine and crumbly tilth, tread it down with small sideways steps back and forth then rake some more.

3. Mark out straight rows with lines of string tied tight between two sticks. Onion sets require planting at 15cm intervals with 30cm between rows. Work from wooden planks if the soil is wet.

4. Press each set carefully into the soil but leave the top half exposed. Firm gently with thumb and first-finger knuckles. Check daily for a week. Reposition any that have worked loose or become displaced. Keep moist, weed-free, then watch and wait.

Tending Celeriac

Celeriac is coming along beautifully. The stems are currently tennis ball-sized, creamy-beige as they stand proud and swollen above the dark, loamy soil. All of my family are rather partial to this easy-to-grow alternative to celery. Alablaster is a reliable variety, providing a knobbly, pock-marked harvest throughout the winter from a sowing made in March.

This week I've been tending the crop, hand weeding in amongst them and removing the lower leaves. These have a tendency to droop and flop onto the soil. Not only does this look shoddy but it also provides a sheltered hiding place for slugs and snails right where they are not wanted. These voracious molluscs don't need a second invitation to commence chomping on celeriac. Hence, to keep the veggies clean and in tiptop condition, I advise getting rid any sagging foliage with a careful, gentle, downwards tugging rip. Strappy and deep green, the leaves part easily in this condition with a crunching tear, releasing a strong celery-like aroma. The smell is identical to

SEPTEMBER WEEK 2
JOBS TO DO THIS WEEK

IN THE GREENHOUSE
- Ventilate.
- Water tomatoes, aubergines and peppers once every three days with liquid feed added.
- Keep cabbages moist but not wet.

ON THE PLOT
- Water strawberries in pots.
- Continue to dig Maincrop potatoes.
- Pick beans regularly, every day if possible.
- Wash pots to prevent a massive job later.
- Plant out Ormskirk Savoy cabbages into rich ground.
- Clear spent cucumber plants.
- Place newspapers under and around tomato plants. Untie from their supporting canes and lay them on the paper for fruits to ripen but stay clean.
- Compost exhausted dwarf French beans.
- Plant potted blueberry bushes into soil enriched with ericaceous compost, or large pots of similar.
- Don't let your hoe lie idle in dry weather - keep it busy and sharp.

their taste, reminiscent of roasted Sunday feasts and Mrs Nails' warming winter soups. These pleasant thoughts are more than enough to inspire me into doing a thorough and proper job, in drooling expectation of the dinner-time delights to come from next month onwards.

September

Making a Pond

I spent a day this week digging a pond for the vicar because she loves wildlife and frogs especially. It's quite a strenuous task, demanding plenty of back work and humping soil in a wheelbarrow. However, Young Master Nails was fortunately on hand, willing to roll up his sleeves and get stuck in. He helped to lighten the load enormously. This is the last job which we will engage in together for a while. The strapping young man moves to the city at the weekend to commence a new life studying and furthering his career in music.

Ponds are hugely beneficial and attractive to wildlife, especially when one of the sides at least has shallow margins. They are welcome as watering holes for birds and badgers, provide breeding opportunities for frogs, toads and newts, and have an almost magnetic pull amongst a range of fascinating insects and creepy-crawlies who will move in of their own accord and make a pool home.

It is not only the garden ecosystem which is enhanced by this wealth of diverse new life but the human residents also. Sitting by a body of water can be a genuinely mellowing and calming experience, whether enjoyed alone in reflective contemplation or with company, chatting and passing time with friends. And almost without exception, children are drawn to the mystery and wonder of underwater life. Such curiosity can spark and stimulate a lifetime of interest in and care for the natural environment and its inhabitants. This is something which I think we should all be fostering in the up-and-coming generations.

Ponds can be constructed with a flexible, non-porous membrane or purchased as a pre-formed, rigid plastic mould. I favour the latter, on account of the fact that these are more robust and long-lasting. Although more expensive, this extra cost is compensated for by the fact that they are virtually puncture proof. For instance, enthusiastic dogs won't breach the bottom when they dive in for a wallow and drink (which they are apt do). They are also less of a fiddle to fit.

Somewhere which is not overhung by trees and has access to sunshine for at least part of the day year-round is ideal. A hole needs to be created which can receive the mould snugly. To this end, scratch the outline of your pond in the soil and, starting at one end, commence to dig. Insert the spade to a depth of one spit (the length of the flat end) and remove the earth to a barrow. Work methodically in rows from left to right moving backwards, in much the same way as one reads down the page of a book.

With the surface area of the pond dug thus, a shovel is usefully employed to clear loose debris and make a clean, sunken surface. The same technique is repeated, digging to the depth of a second spit, then a third and so forth, until a hole the desired dimensions has been excavated. This is actually the easy bit as settling the pond in to a level and flush fit requires much 'fine tuning'.

Get rid of any stones and smooth over rough edges. A 2.5cm thick carpet of sand at the bottom and on horizontal shelves will cushion the weight when filled and afford a bit of adjustment and 'give'. A small amount of water in the mould indicates when a level has been found, at which point careful infilling of the sides and gaps with loose soil can take place. This should be done firmly but not so as to cause the plastic sides to be pushed inwards. It is a job which is best done as the pond is being filled with a hose pipe, to keep a constant check on the level. Once full, leave it alone for a few days. Tap water contains additives and chemicals which are not particularly conducive to aquatic plants and animals. These must be allowed time to evaporate off. In a week or so, stocking with plants can begin!

Two words of warning. Firstly, if toddlers are in the area, they must be denied access to the edges with a barrier so that they cannot fall in. Secondly, if your pool is ultimately for wildlife and not purely ornamental, do not stock with fish. They will eat lots of beneficial and interesting creatures, including tadpoles.

SEPTEMBER Week 3: SOWING CORN SALAD

1. Corn salad, also known as lambs' lettuce, is a small but hardy plant. It can be cultivated for late winter and early spring salads. 'Broadcast sow' seeds by scattering on any spare patch of soil before raking in.

2. Seedlings develop happily enough with or without protection from the elements. Corn salad grows wild in the UK. Dry, sandy soils are preferred. In places it may be a common weed.

3. Deployment of protection in the form of horticultural fleece or plastic bells will hasten growth. Using these techniques brings corn salad into cropping condition earlier.

4. Leaves can be picked individually for a garnish. Whole plants may be teased from the soil, dunked in water to wash and have roots trimmed before being presented whole on a plate or in sandwiches.

SEPTEMBER WEEK 3

JOBS TO DO THIS WEEK

IN THE GREENHOUSE

- Ventilate.
- Harvest last of the tomatoes then remove and burn plants.
- Water lettuces and cabbages yet to be planted out.
- Compost spent aubergine plants.
- Sow D'orlanda corn salad and winter purslane.

ON THE PLOT

- Tidy away unused bamboo canes.
- Wash pots.
- Water potted carrots.
- Keep digging Maincrop potatoes.
- Paint wooden sheds with preservative.
- Plant out Tiger lettuces.
- Plant out more Myatts Compacta cabbages.
- Mulch ground between cabbages with newspaper and grass clippings.
- Check over all areas.
- Deadhead butterfly bushes around plot edges to stimulate more flowering.

September WEEK **4**

Over-Wintered Red Electric Onions

Slightly later than usual, this week I've been planting onion sets. Electric is a red variety available in garden centres now. They will over-winter quite happily from an autumn planting, establishing strong root systems and healthy, green, top growth over the next three or four months. All being well, come springtime, after having had a rest at New Year the little onions will plump up and mature for a summer harvest some two/two and a half months in advance of the main crops which, having been planted in March, will have not long been in the ground and are still playing catch up.

Red onions are particularly flavoursome and good for you when taken raw, thinly sliced in salads. They add colour and depth in almost any dish to which they are added. I enjoy them most when cooked slowly to the point of caramelisation, whereupon their rich sweetness is an onion lover's delectation that can be enjoyed with relish.

Red onions do not keep as well as whites and are thus more of a seasonal pleasure, but nurturing appropriate varieties in both spring (Red Baron for example) and autumn ensures that they are available in the kitchen as much as possible.

Firm, but not compacted, ground is desirable in the cultivation of onions. To achieve this remove every weed by forking over the plot selected for this crop. After that, employ the 'gardener's shuffle' to settle the soil. This involves taking small, sideways, mini-steps over the surface until the whole area has been gently trodden over. It is then raked to a crumbly tilth on top and the whole process repeated in readiness for planting. Rows are marked out with canes and string 30cm apart. If the land is sloping, it makes good gardening sense to always establish your rows across the angle of the dip and not with it. This reduces surface water run-off with the added advantage of lessening the risk of soil erosion during heavy winter rains.

Place the marble-sized Electric sets along these rows at 15cm intervals first, then work back, nestling each one 2.5cm or so deep into a soil pocket which is made by pushing a finger into the moist medium. Leave the top half standing proud.

Take time and care to individually firm them into the ground without damaging the bulbs. This is crucial because when the roots do commence to grow (in only a matter of days) they are apt to push the tiny onions up and out of their nests. This is a likely explanation as to why they are often found lying on their sides out of line on top of the soil over the next week or two. Having said that, birds will sometimes tug at the tips during the course of looking for a meal and errant cats are always wont to use any freshly worked patch of bare soil for their ablutions. Dislodged or loose onions simply need to be replaced and/or re-firmed as before with a watchful eye kept on them daily until emerging green shoots indicate that beneath, roots are well anchored. Subsequently, tend them by keeping moist and weed free (easy to do in the winter), and wait patiently.

SEPTEMBER WEEK 4
JOBS TO DO THIS WEEK

IN THE GREENHOUSE
- Water seeds.
- Tidy up.

ON THE PLOT
- Dig Maincrop spuds.
- Hand weed amongst leeks.
- Remove outer leaves from celeriac.
- Plant winter Radar and red Electric onion sets.
- Harvest Butternut squashes.
- Mow grass paths.
- Trim edges.
- Keep the hoe busy.

SEPTEMBER Week 4: AN EXPERIMENT WITH BEANS

1. An interesting experiment with beans for children of all ages requires two pint glasses, toilet paper or kitchen towels, water and a few runner and climbing French bean seeds.

2. Stuff the glasses with paper and make it damp. Push the seeds halfway down the sides against the glass. Keep in a sunny place. Observe their germination in progress daily.

3. Runner beans split open. A shoot pushes up from within the two seed halves, called 'cotyledons'. They remain underground. French beans develop differently. Their cotyledons arch up and out into fresh air on top of a shoot, then break open to reveal the leaves inside.

4. A simple activity like this is fun and educational. It can inspire a life-long interest in the natural magic of growing plants for future generations of budding gardeners.

September

Veg on the Menu

Leaves and greens
Cabbage
Calibrese
Leaf beet
Swiss chard

Roots, tubers and stems
Beetroot
Carrots
Potatoes, Second Early and
Maincrop

Salads
Land cress, American

Onion tribe
Garlic
Onions
Red onion
Shallot

Beans, peas and pods
Borlotti beans
Bush beans, Hesta
French beans
Runner beans

Vegetable fruits
Chilli pepper
Corgette, Yellow Straightneck
Squash, Spaghetti
Tomatillo, Verde
Tomato

Fruit and nuts
Apple, Scrumptuous
Apple, Sunset
Cobnut, Nottingham
Pear, Beth
Pear, Conference

Cereal
Sweetcorn

October

Stocking the Pond

This week I've been stocking a pond which Young Master Nails and I constructed a couple of weeks ago for a friend. Rather than doing it immediately upon settling-in the lining and filling, it is wise to allow a few days' interim for treated tap water to stabilise and balance. This done, the time soon comes for introducing aquatic and semi-aquatic vegetation which looks pleasing, brings the pond to life and inevitably brings in some lower animal species. The ongoing ecological development of plant and animal communities is thus given a kick start.

To this end, look no further than already established ponds existing in your own garden or those of your neighbours. Mine are still throbbing and heaving with thick mats of waterweed, clumps of sword-like yellow flag iris and expansive lily pads which both sit flat on the water surface and loll above it like great rolling tongues fighting for a bit of space to flop down and spread onto. Beneath the surface, all manner of real-life dramas are being acted out by a myriad of small and microscopic creatures which live lives so far removed from our human experiences that they are almost beyond comprehension. That said, it is this self-contained wonder world which us wildlife-friendly gardeners seek to encourage and nurture so, with half-filled bucket by your side, on bended knees with rolled-up sleeves, delve into the cool liquid and select a few prime plant specimens for relocation.

A new pond does not require to be overloaded. A knife can be used to cut portions of matted weed. Plopped in a bucket, this can simply be swilled out into its new home and allowed to establish on its own.

Plants that live partially submerged provide an important bridge for animals such as damselflies and dragonflies that need to spend part of their lives above and part below the water. Having spent a year or more below the surface as voracious predators, they must have something to grab hold of to clamber up and out of the drink. Once in the air, they rest. Their skin splits open along the back and from the protective crispy husk of old they haul themselves free as magnificent, jewel-like winged masters of the air.

Yellow flag iris fits the above-and-below-water bill perfectly and once it has had a couple of years to settle will delight the wildlife gardener with a gorgeous display of unfurling, golden, inside-out petals during early summer. To take a cutting get right in amongst the mud and sludge. Break off a piece of stout stem with leaves attached and place it in a large clay pot packed with a little mud but mostly stones. Put in the new pond as desired. It will happily reside and root in its new container.

For water lilies, there is a selection available

from garden centres and pet shops in a range of colours and adapted to different depths of water. But plunder your own stock if you can, especially if you have the pleasure of overseeing a particularly lovely and persistent specimen. Taking a knife to it down below, sever a sprouted extension of tuberous stem. This can look immediately at home, weighted down at the root end with stones.

Duckweed is a small, single-leaved green plant that grows on the water surface and dangles thread-like roots free in the water. It is apt to multiply in favourable conditions and form enveloping mats. These can be controlled by scooping up handfuls and removing to the compost. As a native, I'm thrilled to have duckweed thriving on all my water habitats.

Canadian pondweed gets a mixed press on account of its vigorous nature. It may choke a small pond. On the plus side, it releases copious amounts of life-giving oxygen into still waters and is easily controlled by just pulling wads onto the side. In a few days, snails, crustaceans and other invertebrates will

have dragged their way back into their watery home. The weed is then another valuable additive to the refuse heap. Canadian pondweed can be allowed to float free in the water or alternatively it can be planted in lattice pots using gravel instead of soil.

The water fern Azolla should be avoided. It chokes ponds with fleshy masses of reddish, scaly, individual, surface-floating leaves. Azolla can spread easily via birds who unwittingly transport this rampant alien introduction on legs and feathers after having a splash and bathe.

Bigger animals, so-called 'mega fauna' such as frogs and newts, will colonise suitable pools in their own time. Only two days after flopping a bucket-load of weed into another new pond next door recently, I heard repeated excited screams and whoops of delight from the young children who had found their first frog. 'Kermit' was resting up, freckled with duckweed, half in and half out of the water. Parents and friends were taken out, one at a time, to admire the handsome fellow!

OCTOBER WEEK 1
JOBS TO DO THIS WEEK

IN THE GREENHOUSE
- Keep ventilated in mild weather.
- Tend to needs of seedlings.

ON THE PLOT
- Dig Maincrop potatoes. Wash and dry before storing one deep in plastic fruit trays.
- Cut comfrey bed and stuff foliage in old wormery to make liquid manure.
- Harvest squashes.
- Weed and clear ground covered by squashes.
- Remove spent climbing French and Borlotti beans to the compost heap.
- Take down poles used as a climbing frame for beans.

OCTOBER Week 1: MULCHING

1. 'Mulching' the veg patch means covering the top layer of soil. Farmyard manure is the best. It feeds creatures in the soil, especially earthworms, protects it and releases vital nutrients for crops. Manure keeps soil warm in winter and conserves moisture during summer.

2. Newspaper and cardboard are considered organic mulches because they rot down readily. They are especially useful when laid down underneath manure as a protective winter blanket.

3. Non-organic mulches include plastic sheeting. It is often left in place for a year or more to kill persistent weeds by totally preventing light penetration.

4. Old carpet is another favourite amongst gardeners. It is a light excluding mulch used to suppress weeds and create bare soil without digging.

October

Harvesting Spaghetti Squash

This is about the right time of year for gathering in your spaghetti squash harvest before the first frosts threaten to nip them. From seeds sown in the greenhouse during mid-April and subsequently planted out on the plot at 60cm intervals as thrusting youngsters in mid-May, hopefully they have thrived.

Spaghetti squash is a reliable and fairly prolific producer of rugby-ball sized, oval fruits. Creeping branches spread out across the ground with up to half a dozen edible pieces per plant. These start off as pale green, hardening to yellowy-cream as they ripen.

Foliage is dying back by October, revealing a scattering of plump, hard and heavy fruiting bodies. I'd advise employing a sharp knife to sever them from the mother plant. Keeping qualities will increase by ensuring that a length of stalk remains attached to each one. Place your haul carefully in a wheelbarrow and remove to the shed or a well-ventilated greenhouse. Spaghetti squashes store well in cool, dry, frost-free conditions.

While Birds Play

The season is unmistakeably on the change. During a session clearing weeds midweek I paused from toiling to stretch my back and admire a many-dozened flock of jackdaws sweeping across the turbulent sky above. Set amid the blustery blue-grey in loose formation, they looked for all the world as if they were having fun, acrobating and dancing with rapid swoops and twisting turns, gliding in synchrony then exploding apart into scattered, smaller units only to regroup and banter elsewhere, wheel around and repeat the game.

In the midst, a couple of ravens, twice as big, surfed the air waves with wings held out to either side, catching currents. Tumbling and soaring, they raced overhead as if chasing the ever-changing clouds, punctuating the windy soundscape of buffeted trees and swirling pressure with unmistakeable deep, gruff, rasping honks and croaks amid the constant chattering of their gambolling, smaller cousins. The larger birds soared in curvaceous glides high overhead, side by side with their jack-ing shadows. Suddenly, the folding of outstretched wing prompted a cork-screwing somersault, raven spinning right round like a stunt plane, then continuing on course as if nothing happened, tracing a route which was imitated by the playful companions.

This animate poetry in motion continued repeatedly for five enthralling minutes. Then, as if by magic and in almost the blink of an eye, the birds were gone from this scene to other places. The skies were empty. I returned my gaze back to earth, plunged in the fork, and continued with the labour of love.

Taking Down French Beans

By now, even though I adore them, I've eaten just about as many climbing French beans as anyone could reasonably be expected to take. Much of the pleasure of growing your own is the seasonality of different foodstuffs. Frenchies are no exception. Having been a delicious and welcome portion on the plate in summer and autumn the time is now right to bid them farewell for another year and move on to other things - parsnips, swede and winter greens for instance.

To this end, I've been taking down my hard-working and productive Blue Lake variety and dismantling the structures which have been supporting them. It's a case of simply snipping the plants off at ground level all along the row and pulling the canes up with bean tops (haulm) twisted around. Twine, used to lash them together, is cut, canes extracted and bundled together for safekeeping until next year. The knotted tangle of stems and leaves is easily spiked with a garden fork and pitched on top of the refuse.

Although initially the compost heap will wear this haulm like a precarious shock of matted green hair, in no time it will have settled down and commenced to transform into compost. In the soil, roots are decomposing too. Being fiercely rich in nitrogen, they will slowly release this essential nutrient which can be tapped into by a subsequent green-leaved crop.

OCTOBER WEEK 2
JOBS TO DO THIS WEEK

IN THE GREENHOUSE
- Ventilate in the mornings.
- Keep seedlings moist but not wet.
- Keep harvesting aubergines before the purple fruits lose their shine.

ON THE PLOT
- Continue to dig Maincrop spuds, wash and store.
- Clean outside leaves off celeriac plants.
- Hand weed here and there.
- Strim or mow all perimeter paths.
- Check over red cabbages for pests.
- Take down outdoor tomato plants. Burn the stems and leaves (haulm) to prevent any over-wintering of disease.
- Check over all stored onions.
- Compost spent pot marigolds. They make useful bulky additions to the compost heap.
- Hoe amongst over-wintering Electric onions.
- Harvest Wagener apples and store in a cool, frost-free place.

OCTOBER Week 2: PURPLE SPROUTING BROCCOLI MAINTENANCE

1. Tend to the seasonal needs of purple sprouting broccoli. Remove all old yellowing foliage and tread down earth around the base of each plant to keep the roots firm.

2. Use a swan-necked, or 'draw', hoe to mound soil up around the base. This 'earthing up' helps steady the plants in the face of battering winter winds.

3. Insert a stout stake at an angle to avoid puncturing the root-ball. Lash it to the stem with baler twine tied into a figure-8 for ultimate wind-proof support.

4. Pigeons love all leafy brassicas, especially during cold spells when there is little else easily available to eat. They peck foliage to smithereens and foul crops with their droppings. Keeping bird-scaring devices in good working order is vital.

October

Apple Day

This is a good week for thinking about apples. Many people have a passion for these most versatile of fruits, not only on account of the many and varied ways they can be eaten, but also because apple trees and orchards provide havens for wildlife and a peaceful oasis for people. Apple trees offer opportunities and are accessible to everyone. Varieties are available which grow into trees of a suitable size for any garden, from pot-grown patio plants on Pixie rootstock, to full blown beauties on M25 rootstock that handsomely grace gardens the size of a small park.

I have a collection of apples in my own garden on M26 rootstock. They are being trained into 'bush' trees. As yet young, they will ultimately reach a height of no more than 3 metres. This both keeps their bounty within reach and makes them ideal for a small plot of land. Next door, a fabulous old Bramley (Britain's most popular cooking apple) commands the garden. An assortment of swings festoon the sturdy branches for kids to play on and a big specimen like that provides the thrill of an exciting tree climb that youngsters find hard to resist.

Just as the French famously grow assorted vines, so the British have selectively bred a kaleidoscope of nigh on 2000 different kinds of apple since Roman times. Each has its own special qualities and virtues for eating, cooking and drinking. Every one of these individual types is descended from fruits borne originally in the ancient mountainous Chinese/Kazakhstan borderlands. The Crab apple is different. It's a thorny native which recolonised our countryside at the end of the Ice Age about 10,000 years ago. The relationship between people and apples dates back to at least this time and Community Orchards represent a contemporary arrangement in this marriage.

It's great to be involved in such a place if one exists in your neighbourhood. This week why not join in the fun and frolics on Apple Day, which falls on or around October 21st every year? Community Orchards provide an outdoor meeting point for locals and visitors to gather, relax, play and share, in the company of nature. Through selecting, planting, nurturing and harvesting, folk of all ages and backgrounds are able to come together, reviving and rekindling an ancient and deep-rooted way of life. Varieties can reflect the soils and environments of the places where they grow as well as the whims and fancies of those who look after them.

Although our Community Orchard is in its infancy and thus not producing any fare yet, generous helpings of apples were gathered and legitimately scrumped in the days leading up to it. Apple Day was a roaring success and a good time was had by all. The children ran Apple & Spoon races, got soaking wet whilst Bobbing Apples, tackled Apples on Strings and smashed hundreds of windfalls with their parents in a boisterous game called Splat the Apple (which is played like rounders, except with a small cricket bat). Meanwhile, the community elders battled it out to produce the Longest Peel whilst chatting, musing, refereeing and watching the organised chaos all around.

Mostly the sun shone although there was a downpour early afternoon when a brief but heavy storm cloud passed overhead, as is the reassuring norm for this time of the year. But spirits were far from dampened. Mrs Nails' chocolate-covered apples on sticks were eagerly consumed by the happy youngsters. Cider and juice, both made locally and the latter produced on the day in front of a fascinated and thirsty audience, refreshed all. As the assembled gradually departed and drifted their separate ways, leaving nothing but footprints in the mud and the acceptable natural litter of dashed and pulverised apple remains scattered about, we were left to reflect on the democratising qualities of communal green spaces.

OCTOBER WEEK 3
JOBS TO DO THIS WEEK

IN THE GREENHOUSE
- Keep an eye on winter purslane and corn salad seedlings for signs of pests or disease.
- Ventilate in the mornings.

ON THE PLOT
- Dig the last Maincrop potatoes.
- Have a big bonfire to get rid of all the non-compostable rubbish.
- Check all veg and fruit in store.
- Mulch rhubarb crown with a thick layer of well-rotted manure.
- Keep the hoe busy if conditions are dry, otherwise do a bit of hand weeding at every opportunity to keep on top of this ongoing chore.
- Remove yellowing lower leaves from Brussels sprouts.
- Check that posts supporting Brussels sprouts are firm and ties secure.

OCTOBER Week 3: HARVESTING WINTER VEGETABLES

1. Sunday is feast day for the family with lots of crops on the menu. A lot of the work on the plot in coming months will simply involve harvesting what is to be eaten on the day.

2. Radishes like these Black Spanish Round are crunchy and hot. Slice thinly for spicy sandwich fillings or grate with carrots to make a warming autumn salad.

3. Hamburg parsley is a thin-rooted variety of the familiar garden herb. Everything is edible. Parsley-flavoured chunks of roasted root go perfectly with pies and mash.

4. Leeks are in season until late March. Digging them for same-day consumption is a thrill in any weather. Fresh leeks have the most wonderful aroma. Trim the roots and leaves before taking indoors.

October

Tending Rhubarb

Some essential late autumn husbandry work with a few of the permanent fixtures in your veg patch should now be addressed. Rhubarb, for example, enjoys a sunny position and basks for much of the day in a prime location. Delicious pink stems are one of the first crops of each new gardening season, offering a sweet-tasting harbinger of summer just-around-the-corner in April. However, by this time of year, the expansive, umbrella-like green leaves are withering to a thin brown mush and those once so-appetising stalks are doing likewise. They come away with barely a tug.

Now is the time to carefully remove any that are well decomposed, add them to the refuse heap, and give the hard-working crown a good boost. To this end, when most of the leaves have finished and there is barely anything to see of this luscious (in summertime) plant, apply a thick mulch of the finest well-rotted manure which was put to one side a few months ago specifically for this purpose. Flop it down right on top and pat down gently into a pancake with the palm of your hand. Over the coming months, as the plant lies dormant underground, rhubarb roots will be able to tap into the goodness that filters down from above, ready for another energetic growing season in the spring.

Caring for Frogs

The extended mild weather of late, which may just have broken midweek, means that frogs who would ordinarily be tucked up deep within the nooks and crannies of stacked wood, piles of stones or other such hidey-holes, have still been very much in evidence as the veg patch is gradually tidied. The working garden presents these useful, pest-eating amphibians with hazards as well as homes.

Buckets left standing around are a case in point, being potential death traps to creatures who leap in and are then unable to get out. I have, on occasion, found one of my wide-mouthed friends drowned and spread-eagled in such a half-full receptacle which is sad for both the little mite and wildlife-friendly gardener. I discovered such a fellow, thankfully still very much alive, trapped at the bottom of an empty bucket on Sunday morning. He was released into the jungle by one of the ponds but this predicament provided a reminder to keep the buckets turned upside-down. Those containing water are routinely made safe by placing lengths of stick or old broom handles as a prop, so that frogs which make a wrong move can easily climb up and out again.

Hauling in the Last Spuds

Growing veggies provides many opportunities for pleasant surprises and the Maincrop potato harvest has certainly been pleasing this year. I like to experiment with a different variety each season and chose Picasso this time around. It's a fine, creamy-fleshed spud, with yellow skin and a red eye. In spite of the fact that there was precious little by way of rainfall throughout the growing period until August and that no additional water was given, they have performed magnificently. The last of the crop was lifted out of the ground this week and now it's a challenge to find enough suitable storage space to squirrel away the bumper haul.

No special treatment was lavished on these spuds, aside from the usual care and attention in the details of cultivation. In this respect, 25cm deep trenches were dug back in the early spring then lined with a spread of compost and partially decomposed farmyard manure. 'Chitted' (pre-sprouted) tubers were nestled into this at 75cm intervals, and covered with 15cm of soil. Regular earthing up with more soil around the leaves (haulm) occurred until late June as the tops grew.

That was it really, with the tatties being left to fend for themselves into mid-August whereupon the dreaded potato blight took hold, prompted by a combination of high temperatures and rain. At this point, removal and burning of the haulms to check this fungal disease was the only option. Harvesting commenced at the beginning of October with super spuds coming up the size of small boulders. Virtually unblemished by either scab or slugs I've made a note to try Picasso again next year, with high hopes for another collection of lovely whoppers.

OCTOBER WEEK 4
JOBS TO DO THIS WEEK

IN THE GREENHOUSE

- Compost the last of the aubergines.
- Keep salads moist but not wet.
- Ventilate freely in fine weather.
- Wash down equipment and generally tidy up. This includes cleaning the glass or clear plastic windows.
- Prick out winter purslane and corn salad into individual pots.

ON THE PLOT

- Clear weeds from areas where veggies have been harvested.
- Take time to stand and stare.
- Pick over the asparagus bed to keep it completely clean.
- Harvest tomatillo plants.

OCTOBER Week 4: CLEANING THE GREENHOUSE

1. Fungal diseases such as grey mould thrive in the warm enclosed conditions of the greenhouse environment. They spread via microscopic spores and can ruin crops such as tomatoes in the space of a few days if not removed promptly.

2. Lots of spiders are resident in the greenhouse by autumn. They do a great pest control job. Before disinfecting stroke each one with a fine brush and catch in a container held underneath as they drop down on a silken thread.

3. Cleaning and disinfecting the greenhouse must be done every year in the interests of health and hygiene. The inside and all contents should be cleaned with a biodegradable disinfectant diluted to the manufacturer's recommendations.

4. Leaves can block gutters and foul water butts. Remove falling foliage and put on the compost heap to become a valuable, soil enhancing resource.

121

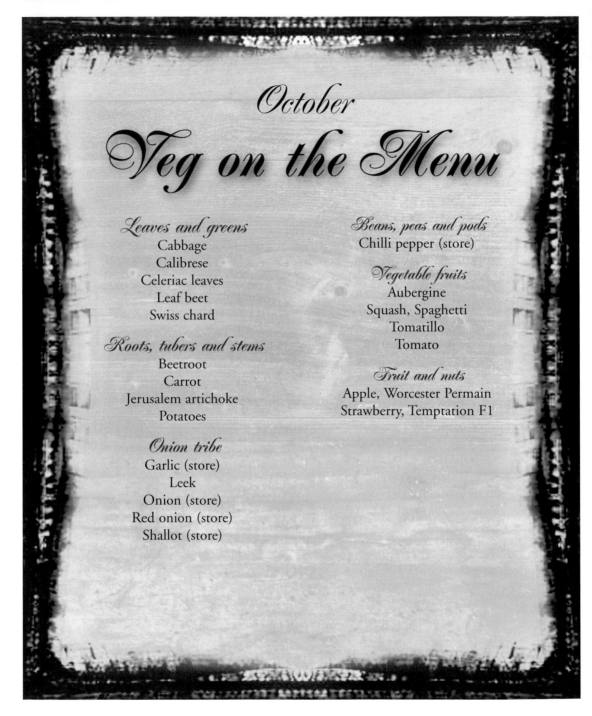

October

Veg on the Menu

Leaves and greens
Cabbage
Calibrese
Celeriac leaves
Leaf beet
Swiss chard

Roots, tubers and stems
Beetroot
Carrot
Jerusalem artichoke
Potatoes

Onion tribe
Garlic (store)
Leek
Onion (store)
Red onion (store)
Shallot (store)

Beans, peas and pods
Chilli pepper (store)

Vegetable fruits
Aubergine
Squash, Spaghetti
Tomatillo
Tomato

Fruit and nuts
Apple, Worcester Permain
Strawberry, Temptation F1

November   WEEK 1

Tending Asparagus

With the onset of winter the feathery plumes of asparagus top growth turn various shades of brown and greeny-yellow. This indicates that their job is done, most of the goodness having been reabsorbed into the underground roots (or 'crown'). Now is the time to put these plants to bed.

Asparagus is a long-term crop, occupying the same piece of land for 15 years or more if well tended and looked after lovingly. Treatment at this time of year is the same whether the bed is in its infancy and has yet to yield a harvest or established and cutting consistently throughout a heavenly six or eight week season in May and June. All that is needed now is a sharp knife or secateurs, a goodly supply of well-rotted farmyard manure and a draw (swan-necked) hoe.

Start by cutting all the strings which have been tied taught between stout posts at the end of each row. These have been supporting the top-heavy asparagus, preventing wind-rock and subsequent damage to the crowns. It is then simply a matter of getting stuck in low down with the secateurs, snipping each stem 2.5cm or so above ground level. Care must be taken to keep to the side and not tread on top of the rows themselves as this can compact damp soil and damage brittle roots that lie not far beneath the surface. A wooden plank serving as a walking board is useful in this respect.

Even a one- or two-year-old bed produces a mass of refuse. Either gathered up in big bear hug armfuls or skewered on a garden fork and carried on the shoulder, this should all be removed to the fire site (not compost heap) in order to destroy pests and diseases, especially over-wintering asparagus beetles.

The appearance of the vegetable patch will be drastically altered by this action, opening it out once more to the elements. I'd take this opportunity to give it a (hopefully) final thorough clean-up of the season, teasing seedling weeds out of the moist soil by hand and with roots intact. On no account should deep-rooted specimens be allowed to remain in place. A hand fork is usefully employed to ease troublesome customers free without disturbing the precious resting crop. It is then a matter of applying a mulch of manure and drawing a little soil over this with the aid of a hoe. The resulting 'ridge and furrow' effect is pleasing to the eye and exactly what this gourmet vegetable needs to maintain peak health.

The First Frost

As if prompted by the change in month, November dawned with the first frost of the winter. This pleases winter veg growers because it heralds the opening of parsnip season. With a 10-metre row of handsome roots in the ground, Mrs Nails and I have much to look forward to. It is by no means essential to wait for freezing temperatures before tucking in to 'snips. However, because starches in this crop are turned into sugars as a result of the low temperatures, they are all the sweeter for it.

NOVEMBER Week 1: JERUSALEM ARTICHOKES

1. Jerusalem artichokes are in season now. Brown woody stems indicate that all the goodness has been reabsorbed into the edible parts below ground.

2. Cut stems down to a few centimetres in height with secateurs. Reduce them further into shorter lengths before consigning to the compost heap. Always use cutting tools with caution to avoid nasty accidents.

3. Jerusalems are notorious for taking over a plot. Sift the soil repeatedly and remove every last fragment while harvesting. The smallest portion will vigorously regrow next spring as a weed amongst other, newly planted, crops.

4. These are the edible underground stems known as 'tubers'. Jerusalems can be very twisted and knobbly. The smooth-skinned variety Fuseau, pictured here, is easy to prepare in the kitchen and provides a delectable, distinctive and creamy alternative to potatoes.

NOVEMBER WEEK 1
JOBS TO DO THIS WEEK

IN THE GREENHOUSE

- Continue sorting and cleaning bit by bit if a whole weekend session is impossible.

ON THE PLOT

- Swaddle wormeries with bubble wrap if the forecast is for freezing weather.
- There is still time to plant autumn garlic.
- Turn over the earth on open areas on heavy soils, or apply a mulch of bulky organic matter to lighter ground.
- Cut down and clear rank vegetation amongst the fruit trees. Keep the bases immediately around the trunks weed free.
- Sow green manures on open plots. Crimson clover is good; it will bind the soil and fix atmospheric nitrogen in the roots.
- Cut down nettles from around the compost heaps.
- Transplant biennial wild flowers that have sprouted in the veg patch, such as foxgloves and great mullien. They will flower next year and be an asset to pollinating insects so make room for them where they won't interfere with edible crops.

November

WEEK 2

Early Winter on the Plot

A little planning and thoughtful spring planting can ensure that your veg patch in the winter is as equally fruitful and productive as it is throughout the summer. Aside from the spuds, squashes, members of the onion tribe and others all safely in store, 'standing' crops which are currently ripe and ready on the plot at this time of year include swedes, celeriac, parsnips, Brussels sprouts, cabbages, scorzonera, salsify, numerous types of kale, chard, leaf beet, Jerusalem artichokes and leeks. Salad is available in the form of self-sown lambs' lettuce scattered all over the place, so-called weeds which actually make rather good eating (such as chickweed) and pinches of herbs courtesy of Mrs Nails' cottage garden.

This week, the last half-dozen beetroots sown last summer were harvested. Beets can be stored for winter consumption in a frost-free environment, packed into boxes of dry sand and kept in the dark. However (and this is a personal thing), I prefer to relish the seasonal sweetness of this easy-to-grow vegetable by punctuating its availability with a time of abstinence. As with many things (broad beans, for example), periods of fast between the feast only serve to heighten the senses and expectation of the home producer.

Onions from store are a real bonus in a hearty dark-season meal. The only problem with them, as far as I'm concerned, occurs in the kitchen. It is the fact that when sliced through with a sharp knife they cause irritation and weeping of the eyes. A tip from my mother solves this phenomenon. She suggests chewing on a hunk of bread whilst preparing these bulbous veggies. It does the job of drying tears magically and is one of those tricks of the trade that works, even though how and why is a mystery to me (in the same way as putting lengths of freshly cut elder in the tunnels of moles will somehow persuade the 'little old man in black velvet' to move from an asparagus bed or flower border and excavate elsewhere).

The weather is a funny thing these days. Driving out from town this week, in spite of it being nigh-on mid-November, the verges and roundabouts had been mowed one morning. The familiar and friendly aroma of freshly cut grass rested somewhat incongruously with the rusty, golden-brown, windswept and slightly bleak urban landscape with its increasingly skeletal trees and drains blocked by wads of browning, rotting leaves. But this is the trend recently, with the purr of lawn mowers a feature of the soundscape ever later in the year.

There are, nonetheless, plus points to the extended hospitable warmth. Despite a few nights of frost and chilly temperatures since the turn of the month, red admiral butterflies are still on the wing. I had great pleasure when observing two of these aristocrats in the garden the other day as I nursed a cup of tea before getting on. The pair were working the marble-sized scarlet fruits of an ornamental weeping

NOVEMBER WEEK 2
JOBS TO DO THIS WEEK

IN THE GREENHOUSE
- Keep the greenhouse ventilated in the mornings.
- Check over salad plants daily.
- Continue to clean and disinfect equipment.

ON THE PLOT
- Sow broad beans Aquadulce Claudia into prepared ground.
- Burn up old asparagus tops.
- On clay soils, dig over open ground and expose it to the elements for winter.

NOVEMBER Week 2: PLANTING GARLIC

1. Garlic is a tough member of the onion tribe and a fairly reliable cropper as long as the ground is not too heavy. Gently prize the bulbs apart into individual cloves.

2. Plunge cloves 6cm deep into weed-free soil, pointed end uppermost. Arrange into blocks or lines with 13cm between each clove.

3. A cold spell immediately after planting is to be hoped for. It stimulates the garlic into dividing and developing strong roots. Shoots should be showing well by New Year.

4. Harvest in summer when the tops are turning brown. Lift them carefully with a garden fork. Hang to dry in a sheltered, airy place. Treated thus, garlic should keep throughout the following winter.

crab apple, uncurling their spring-loaded, coiled tongues to dip and dab for sugars. I was a very happy gardener, admiring them as they flashed their wings open and closed, constantly circling and adjusting, tiptoeing amongst the handsome, shining trusses, like highly-decorated natural ornaments. But they are on borrowed time and must fly south to survive. These beautiful insects are migrants and although they breed here in summer, red admirals rarely, if ever, survived a British winter before the 1990s.

November

Single-Digging

If a golf-ball sized blob of moist (but not wet) garden soil can be kneaded and moulded between the palms of your hands into a glistening sausage that keeps its shape and may even be made into a ring, the growing medium may be described as 'clayey'. The qualities it possesses are different from soils that, for example, are crumbly in the hand and described as 'sandy' (gritty) or 'silty' (smooth). Clayey soils are traditionally referred to as 'heavy', which reflects the effort needed to work them. Drainage can be problematic when compacted, they are slow to warm up in springtime and can bake hard in summer.

However, well-worked clay soils are fertile and often prolific producers of hearty crops. With this goal in mind, heavy soils that are to be put under cultivation next season should be turned over in the early winter to expose them to the elements and let the actions of frost, wind and rain break them down further into a fine tilth for spring sowing.

I am blessed in that my home soils are mostly a dark, fluffy loam that is a pleasure to get stuck into, but times have been when I've had to tame sticky clays for others. These experiences quickly teach that such jobs should be tackled a little bit at a time if one's back (arguably the gardener's most precious commodity) is to be preserved in good health.

Single-digging will do most clay soils the world of good and is far more manageable than the infamously back-breaking task of double-digging, aptly known also as 'bastard trenching'. Double-digging is best reserved for previously unworked plots, or those that have been damaged with machinery or trampling whilst wet.

Single-digging is not complicated. The plot is divided into rows. The first row is excavated down to the depth of a spade head (called a 'spit') and put to one side. Working backwards, the second row is dug out likewise, except that the spoil is deposited into the trench in front. This is repeated, until the last trench to be dug is filled with the soil lifted out initially.

When single-digging it makes sense to take this opportunity to incorporate plenty of organic matter, which will also help to improve the workability of heavy clays. Place compost, well-rotted manure, leafmould or whatever else is to hand at the bottom of each trench before turning the clods behind into it. Adding organic matter thus will also benefit other soil types, providing bulk and body, but is best done in early spring on lighter (sandy or silty) soils. This is because they are more free-draining and can have the goodness washed (or 'leached') out of them by heavy winter rains.

Burning Rubbish

Burning asparagus tops, pruned a fortnight ago, is a fulfilling and important task to do on a Sunday afternoon. In spite of recent cold nights and the lateness of the season a few frogs and toads are still afoot, the mild daytime temperatures keeping them from hibernation. Stacks of vegetable refuse such as asparagus cuttings provide them with a perfect snug hideaway, so always take care when dealing with such waste. Site the fire next to the debris to be burnt rather than under it. Light a pile of scrunched-up newspapers and then heap great forkfuls of the browned and crispy tops onto the flames. If sufficiently dried they go up in a blazing whoosh. In this way, wildlife-friendly gardeners ensure that none of their amphibious allies are accidentally incinerated.

Having a good old burn-up was done under a vast, all-encompassing, fresh-but-blue sky punctuated with barely drifting banks of white fluffy clouds. Some were tight and voluminous, like great bodies of mist surrounding distant mountain peaks, others loose and fragmented, shape-shifting as if by magic, dissipating almost without moving in front of my eyes as I took five to simply stand and stare. Down on the ground, a twisting dance of smoke from the smouldering site curled up as a billowing, heady incense, then raced wildly across the surrounding landscape as a gust caught hold, breathed life into the crackling inferno and carried the plumes away into nothing.

Time spent down on the veg plot at this time of year can be nothing short of paradise. An hour or two in the elements, with bright sun washing over busy gardeners and a brisk wind rushing round their ears, provides an invigorating tonic away from the indoor jobs which must be attended to later. I'm a great believer in getting outside at every opportunity and recharging batteries with some gentle bending and stretching.

NOVEMBER WEEK 3
JOBS TO DO THIS WEEK

IN THE GREENHOUSE
- More tidying and sorting.
- Empty the gutters.

ON THE PLOT
- Keep Brussels sprout plants free of old foliage which might attract slugs and snails.
- Do likewise for cabbages.
- Continue to turn vacant soil.

NOVEMBER Week 3: SUNFLOWERS AND TEASELS

1. Giant Single sunflowers can stand 3 metres or more. In high summer their large heads are incredible gold and brown glories the size of a dinner plate. Bees love them.

2. By November the spent heads are high on the menu for many seed-eating birds, including greenfinches. Leave standing sunflowers for them right through winter, unless adverse weather snaps them first.

3. Teasels are easy-to-grow thistles that bloom the year after sowing ('biennial'). Fragrant purple flowers in July and August are very attractive to long-tongued moths and other insects.

4. At this time of year the spiky, egg-shaped seed heads provide valuable food for birds such as the exquisite goldfinch. Their beaks have evolved perfectly to fit into the depths of these crispy 'hedgehogs' and extract their bounty.

November

Step-over Wagener Apples

Espalier apple trees are specimens that have been trained to grow flat, often against a wall or fence. Tiered branches come off the trunk at regular spaced intervals on the horizontal giving a kind of laddered effect. Where the gardener cultivates an espalier apple tree to just a single tier only 30cm above ground level, and two metres or so either side, it is known as a 'step-over'. It is these that I nurture around part of the veg patch as a decorative yet productive edge for one of the big beds.

To achieve the desired effect, essentially a four-metre baton of living apple wood thick with fruiting spurs along its length, suitable 'spur bearing' varieties must be selected and grown on appropriate rootstock. M27 is the one for step-overs as it is extremely dwarfing and perfect for a tree that is never going to get very big.

Having identified and enriched the planting ground (crucial for dwarfing rootstock), the next job is to secure stout stakes and sturdy, taut wires at the correct distance and height for future training. I'd recommend always purchasing new charges from a reputable nursery as bare-rooted, one-year-old maiden whips. At this stage, they look like short, thin, rooted sticks and are fun to start off because all the subsequent formative pruning and training is in your own hands.

Bare-rooters are best planted during mild and dryish spells between the end of October and beginning of March. Simply make a slot in the prepared plot with a spade, ease down the fibrous roots, tuck them in with flat fingers and then carefully but firmly tread the soil around them to snuggle in the roots and expel any air pockets. Be especially mindful to keep the knuckle-like union between rootstock and named variety (clearly visible, where they are grafted together, just above the roots) free of earth. Planting too shallow or too deep is bound to cause problems later, so go steady and work hard to match the soil mark on the tree with the level of the ground into which it is going.

I planted my young 'uns three winters ago with a stout metal rod for support and at a 45 degree angle in order that the whip could be tied onto the pre-fixed wire and trained along it. The following summer, with wood still young and flexible, a well-placed shoot was chosen for training the other way and eased down in the opposite direction to the leader. Formative pruning since then has involved cutting side growth back after midsummer to five or six leaves from the main branch. In winter, these are further reduced to within two buds of each fruit-bearing 'spur' at the base. This is a job I have been doing this week. The tips are treated similarly. The aim is to bring trees to maximum fruiting capacity after four or five years.

Having a few trees that blossom together in the spring to ensure cross-pollination is the ideal scenario. At least one of my beauties has responded to this regime admirably. It's variety name is Wagener, an old American apple heralding from New York State. Developed for eating (or culinary) purposes, this is a special tree which I cultivate in honour of my mother. Although Canadian-born, she was raised on the US East Coast.

There are many different varieties of apple to chose from. Much pleasure is to be had by anyone who wishes to combine a goodly crop of fruit with a thoughtfully considered named type which adds a personal and/or nostalgic touch to the garden. Arguably, it is this type of individuality which lends to a plot a sense of identity and place in the neighbourhood and wider environment.

Wagener is a hardy and prolific bearer of decent-sized fare. Swelling steadily over the summer months, fruits are ready to pick when cradling the shiny globes in one's hand and uplifting slightly separates them from the tree with ease. This is normally October-time. The great thing about Wagener apples is that they do not ripen until the following January and can be kept crisp and juicy until March. Thus they may be enjoyed at a time of year when home-grown apples are generally considered out of season.

To keep them fit for a mouth-watering early spring snack, store late-season fruit carefully. Now that Mrs Nails has finished her beautiful representation of this season's harvest in oils, the artistically arranged still-life will be dismantled. Each fruit will be lovingly wrapped in newspaper, popped in a plastic tray from the greengrocer and placed on a cool, dry, frost-free shelf in the shed. All being well, they should be fine. Their biggest threat between now and then comes from being discovered, and nibbled, by hungry mice.

NOVEMBER WEEK 4
JOBS TO DO THIS WEEK

IN THE GREENHOUSE
- Ventilate in the mornings.

ON THE PLOT
- Tidy away and compost spent Chevalier calibrese plants.
- Hand weed amongst Jerusalem artichokes.

NOVEMBER Week 4: IN THE VEGETABLE STORE

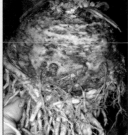

1. Immediately use onions that are sprouting green shoots. Discard any that have gone soft to the compost heap. Be ever watchful around the roots. Early detection of a red slime that oozes from this area is essential. It contaminates others and smells awful!

2. Celeriac can be lifted and stored easily in boxes of dry compost. Alternatively leave this pock-marked, swollen crop in the ground with a covering of straw to protect from frost.

3. Thick-skinned orangey and blue-grey skinned squashes might keep until beyond New Year. Others soften and go mouldy sooner.

4. Rotting potatoes smell truly ghastly. Sniff them and handle gently. Potatoes kept in trays in the dark are easier to check than those stored in sacks, which must be emptied and picked over. Bin or burn bad spuds to prevent the spread of disease.

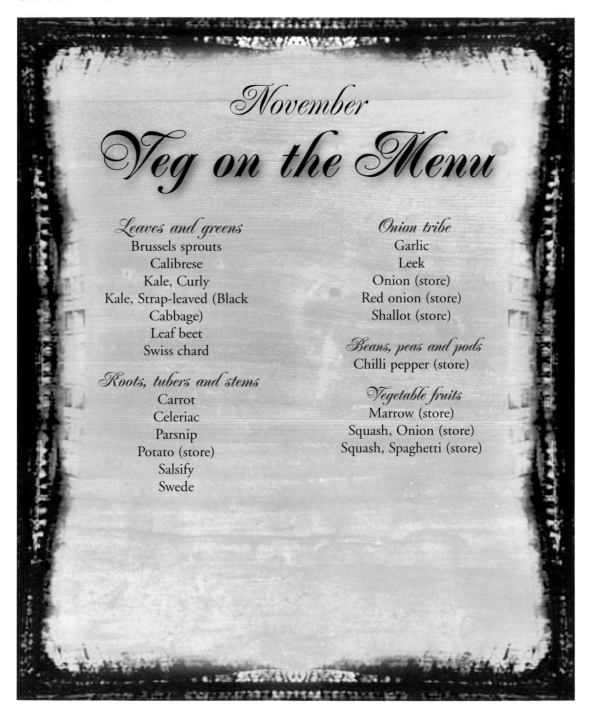

November
Veg on the Menu

Leaves and greens
Brussels sprouts
Calibrese
Kale, Curly
Kale, Strap-leaved (Black Cabbage)
Leaf beet
Swiss chard

Roots, tubers and stems
Carrot
Celeriac
Parsnip
Potato (store)
Salsify
Swede

Onion tribe
Garlic
Leek
Onion (store)
Red onion (store)
Shallot (store)

Beans, peas and pods
Chilli pepper (store)

Vegetable fruits
Marrow (store)
Squash, Onion (store)
Squash, Spaghetti (store)

December

WEEK 1

Soil Management

Along with a strong back, soil is amongst the gardener's most valuable assets. Care and attention lavished on maintenance and upkeep of the growing medium will reap its rewards in the long run as successive harvests of delicious, healthy crops are nurtured from plot to plate. Not only must goodness within the ground be regularly bolstered by the addition of whatever organic matter is to hand, but the surface must also be protected from the erosive powers of wind and rain, especially when veggies are cultivated on a slope.

There are times in the summer when a hot sun can dry out the surface of a light soil to such a degree that it is prone to become dusty and get carried off with the breeze. In the wake of heavy rain, soil can suffer too. Part of my plot is on a south-facing slope and at any time of the year a persistent deluge can prove destructive. One site in particular needs special management in the face of the elements. This was discovered some years ago when first put under the spade.

Having toiled from October to December in meticulous preparation, including removing all the weeds, couch and horsetail to create a lovely fluffy tilth for broad beans sown before Christmas, disaster struck. Prolonged downpours in the early spring spawned flash floods and mini torrents of water coursed across the ground, gouging great rivulets out of the veg patch. A substantial batch of my young broads were either swept away or had their roots laid bare of the good earth which got relocated to clog up a path further down.

This taught me a valuable lesson. Now I never leave this area bare. Plus, I grow crops at right angles to the slope and allow them to stand amongst a light covering of weeds, all of which protects and binds the soil. Cloudbursts of nigh-on biblical proportions can occur at any time during high summer so as and when produce is lifted the weeds are left in the ground to continue their good work - contrary to management on a flat plot.

Then, in early autumn, I clear the bed completely and sow a green manure to see it through winter. Crimson clover is perfect. A fortnight before planting the subsequent crop of my choosing, the so-called 'cover crop' is hoed down and forked in to add nutrients and organic matter.

As intended, by this time of year a few handfuls of crimson clover broadcast sown in September has developed a lush, cushion-like carpet of green leaves. This canopy acts to break up the destructive force of heavy raindrops, filtering them through as a gentle drip-drip. Their extensive roots also knit the soil together, thus saving it from being washed away. In common with all members of the pea family, they are thick with nitrogen-rich nodules down below which will be eagerly tapped into by a subsequent crop of leafy green veg (cabbages, for example, or spinach).

135

DECEMBER WEEK 1
JOBS TO DO THIS WEEK

IN THE GREENHOUSE
- If you have not yet finished cleaning and disinfecting the greenhouse get it done and dusted as soon as possible!
- Ventilate in mild weather.

ON THE PLOT
- Hand weed around plum trees, gages, apples and pears. Mulch each tree with well-rotted manure to a distance of one metre all round the base, but keep the mulch free from touching the trunk.
- Tidy the leaf beet and Swiss chard by removing all the old outer leaves to encourage flushes of fresh growth (protect with a cloche if available).
- Hand weed here and there.

DECEMBER Week 1: DIGGING

1. Digging is a strenuous activity. It is easy to get lost in the rhythmic meditation of this job, which can lead to backache the next day. Don't dig for more than half an hour before taking a break and doing something else.

2. On sloping ground physical effort and erosion can be minimised by facing uphill and working along the contour. With a sensible and realistic approach to digging this annual task may be happily tackled year on year.

3. Robins find rich pickings where soil is disturbed. They drop in fearlessly, hopping from clod to clod, stopping, tilting their heads to one side and listening, then diving into a crack or hollow to snaffle a tasty morsel.

4. Always scrape mud off tools after a session in the veg patch. Clean equipment is much more inviting to use than dirty tools that are caked in mud and will inspire you to do more work on the plot tomorrow.

December

WEEK 2

Tending to the Greenhouse

This weekend I've finally finished sorting out and cleaning the greenhouse. It is a job which would ideally be ticked off during the autumn but work and circumstance have conspired of late to reduce gardening time to a premium, so completion has had to wait until later than usual this year. Truth be told, it is actually rather a pleasant undercover undertaking. Prolonged squalls of unpleasantly heavy, driving rain, repeatedly lashing in almost on the horizontal, have kept me off the plot anyway (for the sake of protecting delicate soil it is sensible to follow the old adage that says if soil sticks to your boots then it is too wet to work outdoors).

I never really put the greenhouse completely to bed because there are always plants being nurtured in the protected environment (at the moment there is just potted-up corn salad, winter purslane, bay cuttings and the citrus trees: lemon and lime). Therefore, shelving is dismantled, removed, cleaned and replaced a little at a time and the same goes for all the pots and other bits and bobs. I have found it easier to do this way because, due to other matters, there was no opportunity for a concentrated two-day splurge before. It has kept the job ongoing and manageable. The entire structure normally gets an internal rub-down and wipe with Jeyes Fluid, but this year I've used a biodegradable disinfectant as a more environmentally-friendly alternative.

Believe me, there is an enormous sense of satisfaction when it is done. The greenhouse is a central hub of activity and vital organ in the living system that is a finely-tuned and fully-functioning fruit and veg garden. Seed-sowing indoors for crops like leeks, early beans, peas and cabbages, will commence as the year turns. A clean and tidy working space makes this proposition an exciting and delicious one.

DECEMBER Week 2: WINTER ONION CARE

1. From a September planting, Radar onions will have established strong roots below which are indicated by good growth on top. They will sit tight for a few weeks now until the warmth of spring urges them on once more.

2. Keeping the onion bed weed-free is important. Employ a kitchen fork to gently tease out unwanted imposters from damp soil.

3. Wood ash from winter fires is a valuable resource. Collect and store in a dry place. It will supply a little fillip to members of the onion tribe when sprinkled in between the rows.

4. Radars plump up encouragingly during April and May. Bulbs can be pulled and eaten two or three months before the main crops, and so are extremely helpful in considerably extending the season.

Tending the Wormeries

I have also been tending my wormeries. I have two on the go in modified water butts. They do a great service in recycling cooked and raw food waste which, laid bare on the compost heap, is a magnet for rats. Chock-full of lovely gubbins and an army of wriggling, squirming worms of the Brandling and Tiger varieties, now is the time to cosy them up and nurse the hard-working fellows through to spring.

Such an important job needs to be done before the cold of winter sets in and has been left a bit late this year on account of the extended mild temperatures. Under more seasonal conditions, this is a late-October operation. However, apart from a week of sharp frosts at the beginning of November, it has continued to be shirt-sleeves weather well into December. With the pivotal Winter Solstice now just days away I'm of the opinion that it surely cannot last (can it?).

DECEMBER WEEK 2
JOBS TO DO THIS WEEK

IN THE GREENHOUSE

- Find a place for all those little essentials like tweezers, dibber and plant identification labels ready for seed sowing in the future.
- Check on potted-up salad plants, but they're unlikely to need watering.
- Ventilate in the mornings if it's fine.

ON THE PLOT

- Potter and tidy. This includes washing dirty pots in a weak mix of water and washing-up liquid.
- Check over all areas.
- Hand weed amongst the Alpine strawberries.
- Keep plot edges weed-free and neat.
- Tie kale plants securely to stout stakes to prevent wind-rock.
- Keep Brussels sprouts plants clean by removing oldest, tattiest, lowest foliage.
- Prepare a fresh planting site for Jerusalem artichokes by digging a trench one spit (a spade head) deep and lining with a mix of well-rotted manure and spent potting compost.
- Hand weed the winter onions.

To this end, swaddle wormery bins with insulating sheets of bubble wrap as a protective plastic blanket loosely secured with string. Attention must be paid to the fact that the worms still need to breath, so don't wrap it tight. Allow for a free flow of air during and after this operation. The industrious little fellows appreciate such care and attention to their needs as they won't work if the medium falls below 15 degrees centigrade.

December

WEEK 3

Fruit Tree Maintenance

Tending young fruit trees is an important job and one which you can see to this week unless conditions are freezing, in which case it is best for the trees to wait for a milder break. In their formative years especially, apples and pears are well cared for if an area of clear soil is maintained for about 60cm around the circumference of the stem. In this way, they are able to gain access to available water and nutrients in the soil without having to compete with other plants which demand the same. As with people, trees which are well catered for in their youth stand every opportunity of making fine specimens when fully grown.

To this end, use a small border fork to delicately and lightly loosen and lift the weeds that have begun to establish in the close vicinity of your trees. With feathery roots often close to the surface, it is a job which must be executed carefully. Accidentally hooking or snapping them will not do the saplings any favours for, while all on top appears to be dormant and inactive, the roots are still busy working hard down below to sustain life. They are constantly extracting what is needed from the surrounding earth and incorporating this elixir into the body of the tree. It is best to leave them as undisturbed as possible.

Just insert the fork prongs (tines) down a little bit and lever them up slightly. Dislodged weeds can be eased out of their cold and moist bed by hand with a firm grip and tug. The cleaned soil must be firmed again with the sole of a boot and a thick mulch of well-rotted manure applied to the base of each tree. Spread your mulch to cover the area of weeded ground and (importantly) keep it just clear from touching the stem. This will supply everything that your top-fruiters need in terms of food and nutrients. When each budding youngster has been similarly treated it will be a job well done and leaves the orchard looking as pretty as a picture.

Mealtime Magic

There is little which can compare with the pleasure to be had from sallying forth into the kitchen garden or down the allotment on a Sunday morning at this time of year and spending a good hour or so gathering the ingredients for a big meal. In the company of distant pealing church bells it's a chance to ruminate and ponder on the successes and failures of the season just passed and enjoy that quiet stillness which comes when winds subside and a timeless magic descends on the neighbourhood once more. This is pottering at its finest, with food in the ground and plenty of opportunities to stand and stare, no need to rush and tear.

Home-grown veggies demand time to prepare in the harvesting, rubbing, scrubbing and washing which precedes delivery to Mrs Nails' kitchen. After admiring and discussing what is soon to be eaten, the odd bad bit must be removed and the produce readied for eating. This cannot be rushed, in the same way that cultivating a tempting row of swedes is not a venture to be entered into in a hurry, when done with love.

I'm a busy man and always have been. 'Burning the candle at both ends,' my mother used to say some years ago. But growing veg is the perfect antidote to this. It reins one in to the natural rhythmic cycle of the seasons. We gardeners work with forces which are so beautifully honed that careful planning and a little forethought can reap plentiful rewards even now, in the so-called 'dead' of winter. Sharing the bounty at mealtime, either with the children who are back home for the festive season, with friends, or both, is a family ritual that has provided my household with some of its finest moments. There is nothing quite like a healthy hunger and the promise of good grub to bring folk together.

DECEMBER WEEK 3
JOBS TO DO THIS WEEK

IN THE GREENHOUSE
- Ventilate a little in the mornings.
- Check over.
- Little else to do so just relax!

ON THE PLOT
- Weed swedes and remove any rank or decaying foliage to the compost heap.
- Store wood ash from fires in a dry container for later use.
- Tie in branches of Morello cherry to supporting framework against a north-facing shed wall.
- Tie in Brown Turkey fig being trained as a fan against a south-west facing shed wall.
- Clear along plot edges.
- Burn up rubbish.
- Harvest selections of veggies to make presents for family and friends.
- Take time in the harvesting away from the rush and tear of the season.

DECEMBER Week 3: ALLOTMENTS

1. Laws were passed in 1845 to legally secure cheap and accessible allotments. They enabled peasants and the 'labouring poor' to grow their own food.

2. Allotments of a practical size for purpose (feeding the family) became established and popular, especially in urban areas. In 1919 and 1945, immediately following the two World Wars, well over a million plots were in active service.

3. Modern sites are havens for folk of all races, ages, genders, political persuasions and classes: individuals who seek solace in the company of the soil and what it can produce.

4. If you fancy getting an allotment, first visit your local council offices and register your name. Depending on the mood of the day, an opportunity to get deep down and dirty may come along sooner than you think. Be prepared.

December

WEEK 4

Tending Greens

This week I've been weeding and cleaning on the plot. Heavy and prolonged rains of late have temporarily quelled and it has been possible at last to get on the land and do some work. This is a relief, because it is all too easy to let a well-tended patch become scruffy and unkempt, which can feel discouraging. The never-ending growing season for weeds makes upkeep sessions a year-round occupation although things are definitely considerably slower as the year draws to a close.

There is a lot of hard graft involved in cultivating your own produce but the truth is that, once the initial ground clearance has taken place, doing a little and often is enough to keep even a fair-sized garden or allotment ticking over and supplying ample food. The weather may not be at its fairest right now, and the days are frustratingly short, but there is still a fine old time to be had bending your back in the company of liquid-noted robins and a steely-grey sky.

Greater spotted woodpeckers have even commenced their drumming, which is a few weeks earlier than usual. The hushed purr of occasional passing traffic in the street, harsh staccato 'pinking' of cat-wary blackbirds and hum of light aircraft overhead is punctuated with the woodpecker's knocking repeat. This evocative sound resonates intermittently from neighbouring woodlands as both sexes proclaim their territories and state their forthcoming intentions to each other. For the happy gardener, midwinter is an opportunity to do as much, or as little, as he or she pleases.

Leaf beet and Swiss chard are by nature biennials, which means that they would ordinarily flower in the second summer after sowing if left to their own devices. What this means in terms of harvesting greens is that an ongoing harvest can be promoted throughout a mild winter by removing old, tough, outer leaves and picking the fresh, pale, younger ones regularly for dinner. It's a job that can be done now. Clean around your plants, twist and yank unwanted brown and holey foliage from low down then remove it to the compost heap. If freezing conditions threaten, a cloche positioned over the crop will offer welcome protection.

Tending Onions in Midwinter

Over-wintering Electric onions should be coming along nicely. After being nestled down as sets at the beginning of October in regimented rows, mine have been virtually untouched since then. Long green shoots, standing erect but lolling at the ends, indicate that all is well. Now is the time to get in amongst your charges, taking advantage of the moist soil to extract all weeds from the vicinity. No tools are needed, just a supple and strong set of fingers to tease the impostors out, roots and all. Even tenacious dock and dandelion come out with root intact at the seedling stage in the right conditions, which is most satisfying. Working along wooden boards saves the soil from compacting underfoot by spreading your weight and enables an industrious gardener to get the job done when others might chose to leave it for another day.

As I took a moment to straighten up and survey the scene, a pair of partridges exploded from behind an adjacent hedge and passed overhead so close that the birds made me jump with alarm at their sudden flurry and whirr. They were of the 'red-legged' variety, game birds which were first recorded as introductions from France in the late 1600s and became an established fixture in the open countryside a century or so later.

The beautifully plump-breasted, stripy-flanked couple glided across the plot and alighted on the bare earth where asparagus is grown before strutting jauntily across to the recently tended rows of greens. Cutworms were their target. They snatched large numbers of the fat brown or green grubs which had been disturbed and exposed by my recent thinning-out session.

Cutworms are responsible for damage to veggies by munching the leaves and roots of various crops. On the plus side, however, they mature into some of our commonest and most beautiful summertime moths such as the Yellow Underwing. There is plenty of room and food for all in an ecologically balanced, chemical-free garden. As I always tell Mrs Nails and the children when a caterpillar turns up in the kitchen, 'If it's good enough for the insects, it's good enough for us!'

DECEMBER WEEK 4
JOBS TO DO THIS WEEK

IN THE GREENHOUSE
- Check over.
- Little else to do.

ON THE PLOT
- Prepare and plant shallots.
- Tend kale plants by stripping yellowing and browning leaves and composting.
- Revamp bird scaring devices: strings, tinfoil and plastic bags tied in the vicinity.
- Mooch around looking for early signs of spring.

DECEMBER Week 4: SHALLOTS

1. Shallots are traditionally planted on the shortest day. Grow them in a sunny bed, raked level and trodden firm, at 23cm intervals in rows 30cm apart. Press each one into the soil gently to half its depth. Check daily until the roots have taken anchor.

2. Shallots are generally reliable and problem-free. However, grazing animals such as rabbits sometimes nibble the aromatic shoots in springtime, as shown above. Barriers might need erecting as a precaution.

3. Pull shallots on or after June 21st in dry and sunny weather, when tops are browning at their ends. Insert a fork diagonally beneath the cluster and lever up slightly to loosen the soil. Grasp the withering greenery and shake free.

4. When ripe the multiple bulbs break apart freely. Rub off excess soil by hand. Lay them on a slightly elevated wire netting frame to dry out completely in the sun. They store well in a ventilated, frost-free place when skins and tops are completely crunchy brown and flaky.

December

Frost

Lately we've been enjoying some thick, lingering fogs and a beautiful series of frosty days which have marked the run up to New Year. On occasions when the pea-souper freezes overnight, a twinkling, cut-glass silvery hoar greets emerging gardeners as they make their way up the garden path in the early morning. The crystal coating grants intimate insight into the twists, turns and distinctive delicacies of form exhibited by different plant species.

A good, hard frost is to be welcomed. As well as casting a beautiful blanket that crunches underfoot in the shadow of hedges and exposes every ridge, furrow, upturned clod and subtle variation of the land, it is extremely useful. Real cold weather is as much a tonic on the plot as stimulating summer sunshine. Forward thinking keeps damage to a minimum. Any losses are evened out by the invigorating actions and consequences of a good old freeze up.

Soil water expands as it solidifies in response to plummeting temperatures, then contracts upon return to a fluid state. This freeze/thaw process permeates into the sods and particles, shattering them as a result and is especially useful in taming heavy clays. A winter's worth of such freezing and thawing will create a fine, fluffy tilth on rough-dug ground without any assistance. A rake can then be usefully employed to level and grade it into a seedbed ripe for sowing come the spring.

Insect damage is reduced too. Turning the earth prior to a bout of chilly weather exposes undesirables not only to the elements but also to the hungry predations of foraging birds.

Wireworms are the tough, orange larvae of click beetles which spend four or five years living off decaying vegetable matter and plant roots. Leatherjackets feast on roots too, as chunky, brown-grey maggots with rippling, segmented bodies. They are immature crane-flies (Daddy-longlegs), and are laid in batches of up to 300 eggs per female. Larval cockchafers (May bugs) are slightly disconcerting - fat, creamy-white, C-shaped grubs with an orange head and legs. During the three or four years they spend feeding in the soil they can do much damage, especially to cereals and grasses. Wildlife-friendly gardeners are generally happy to tolerate the subterranean munching of these (and others) to a degree, but the natural pest control service offered by robins, blackbirds and various insect eaters is something we should always be keen to encourage.

Some crops need protection from the elements. Slightly tender specimens like globe artichokes appreciate a protective mulch of straw or bracken applied around their base. This keeps the worst of any chill off the all-important crown. Emerging rows of November-sown broads beans will benefit from a tunnel cloche being placed over the top if conditions threaten to be severe. The same can be done for Swiss chard and leaf beet, to keep a small but steady supply of greens on the go.

In an unheated greenhouse, single sheets of newspaper spread over trays of seedlings and young plants should suffice. In really cold weather I suggest that you light a slow-burning candle overnight and place it safely on the floor beneath a clay flower pot. It will radiate just enough warmth to keep frosts at bay.

Photographic and written accounts of extracting leeks and parsnips from deeply-frozen ground with crowbars and pickaxes seem incredible in this day and age but give a clue as to the genuine ruggedness of winters that passed not so very long ago. However, the worst may be yet to come. January and February often serve up the most unsociable weather of the year.

DECEMBER WEEK 5
JOBS TO DO THIS WEEK
TAKE A WELL-EARNED BREATHER.

DECEMBER Week 5: MULCHING WITH BRACKEN

1. Bracken insulates tender crops against frost. It can save veggies such as leeks and parsnips from being locked in to frozen soil. Bracken is freely available and sustainable. Use shears to cut supplies from common land and hillsides.

2. Rake cut bracken into piles before stuffing into old compost bags. Stems can splinter painfully so always wear gloves when handling.

3. Spread thickly over and around rows of productive standing crops. A protective bracken blanket applied around the base of globe artichokes should keep crowns safe until spring.

4. People have employed bracken since prehistoric times as bedding, fuel, building material, in potash and detergent production, glass and soap making. Modern gardeners use it on the plot where it will rot down in time to become a fine soil-enhancing compost.

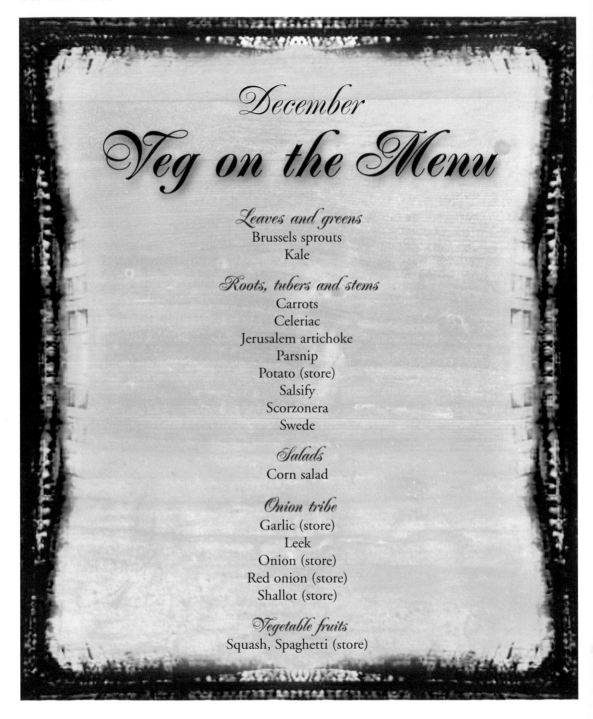

December
Veg on the Menu

Leaves and greens
Brussels sprouts
Kale

Roots, tubers and stems
Carrots
Celeriac
Jerusalem artichoke
Parsnip
Potato (store)
Salsify
Scorzonera
Swede

Salads
Corn salad

Onion tribe
Garlic (store)
Leek
Onion (store)
Red onion (store)
Shallot (store)

Vegetable fruits
Squash, Spaghetti (store)

January   WEEK **1**

Red Mason Bee

This is a good time for thinking about insects and the crucial role they play in keeping the plot ticking over. Bees in particular are integral to the success or failure not just of the kitchen garden but also to the survival of the wider countryside and life as we know it. There are numerous species of these social and solitary insects and none are more useful to home producers than the Red Mason bee (*Osmia rufa*). These industrious little fellows really are the unsung heroes of many a productive plot. Crops that depend on flowering to produce a cache of nutritious food will be serviced by their endeavours, from cucurbits (courgettes and cucumbers) to peas, beans and all manner of fruit.

Purpose-built nests are available from specialist firms and good garden centres. They consist of a plastic cylinder which contains specially-designed cardboard straws, typically 30 or 100, and it is each one of these that provides a potential nursery for the young bees. Such contraptions imitate naturally occurring nesting sites. In the wild these include hollow plant stems and beetle holes in wood. Red mason bees are commonly seen in the vicinity of old walls and outbuildings during the spring and summer months, where they can be observed passing in and out of little passages in the masonry.

Contrary to popular belief, however, they are not responsible for excavating these cavities themselves. The mining work is largely done by the solitary, white-banded 'Davie's colletes', one of eight UK species of Colletes bee. The red mason simply cleans out and renovates suitable sites in the crumbly mortar of old brick and stonework (empty nail or vine-eye holes are another favourite). They lay their eggs in self-sufficient enclosed chambers which they construct and furnish within.

Proprietary nests secured to a south or west-facing fence or shed at or above chest height, in place from the end of February/early March, are sure to attract mason and leaf-cutter bees on the wing in early spring.

Red masons are busy in low temperatures when bumblebees hunker down and remain inactive. Their peak period for useful toil coincides with blossom time for a wide range of top-fruit (apples, pears and plums), and I have heard that one red mason is reputed to do the equivalent pollination of 140 honey bee workers. With no sting (they don't produce honey, so have no need to defend their stores) they are also perfectly safe and harmless in the garden and around children.

Dreaming

This is the perfect time of year for planning not only what to cultivate in the months ahead, but also how to attract an array of beneficial wildlife onto the plot. I've been doing both of these things this week.

Flitting through favourite seed catalogues is always a pleasure as January dawns. With New Year, for me suddenly everything becomes that much more tangible. Spring really is not too far distant. Seeds of a few appropriate veg varieties can be sown from hereon in, leading to a crescendo of activity during March and April.

This is an opportunity for indulgent dreaming. I highlight everything which I plan to grow in the next twelve months then rummage through the box of leftover seeds from last year. Empty packets get discarded but those with practical amounts of viable seed (noted by checking the 'sow by' date on the back) are retained. Many of these will be old favourites. Money can be saved by using these seeds rather than buying new this time around.

JANUARY Week 1: SOIL TEXTURE TESTING

1. Testing whether your soil is sandy, loamy or clayey will assist planning what crops to cultivate and how best to manage your ground. Massage a golf ball sized lump of soil with water so it is uniformly moist but not soaking.

2. Soil moulds into a ball only before breaking apart: sandy. Properties: free draining, rapid nutrient and moisture loss, quick to warm in spring and cool in autumn. Good for root crops. Digging in bulky organic matter, such as rotted manure, will add body.

3. Sausage only: loamy. Properties: warms up quickly in spring, comfortable to cultivate, retains moisture and nutrients well without becoming saturated. Ideal for most types of veg. Feed the soil with annual addition of bulky organic matter.

4. Ring shape: clayey. Properties: heavy to dig, retains moisture and nutrients well, slow to warm in spring for direct seed sowing, bakes hard and cracks in dry weather. Good for cabbages. Add bulky organic matter, grit and sand to lighten clods.

JANUARY WEEK 1
JOBS TO DO THIS WEEK

IN THE GREENHOUSE
- Check over.
- Pot up one tomato seedling which survived the winter.
- Sow sweet pea seeds in trays.

ON THE PLOT
- Have a good mosey round to see what's what.
- Check recently-planted shallots and re-firm as appropriate.
- Clean round the edges.
- Hand weed around Nine Star Perennial broccoli.
- Weed and clear around standing Jerusalem artichokes.
- Prune apple and pear trees unless the air temperature is freezing, in which case delay until the temperature rises.
- Clear soil in vicinity of step-over apples.
- Wassail fruit trees with cider and toast for a (hopefully) bumper harvest this coming season.
- Weed amongst kale.

January WEEK 2

Allotments

This week I've paid my allotment fees. For a very reasonable sum I am able to continue the cultivation of enough ground to feed my family each year. Both Mrs Nails and I never cease to be amazed and thrilled by the range of crops and monies saved by growing our own food.

The history of allotments dates back to at least 1066, and the feudal system established by William the Conqueror. In those long-ago days, ruling gentry lorded it over their serfs who were allowed to cultivate strips of land in the open manorial fields, alongside meadow and grazing rights.

Field enclosures in the 1500s removed some of these rights. A hundred-odd years later, slave-driven workers had been re-classified as peasants. As part of their meagre ration, they were permitted to grow foodstuffs next to their tied cottages in veg patches known as 'pottagers'.

The next wave of enclosure occurred between 1760 and 1818. Open and common land was grabbed on an enormous scale. During that time, five thousand Acts of Parliament secured seven million acres into private ownership. A further seventeen million acres were simply taken, principally by the landed gentry and yeoman farmers.

Peasants were now the 'labouring poor'. Some parish and private ground was rented out to those folk for veg production but opposition to the needs of the workers was rife. Consequently, land allotted for such purposes was few and far between. Where it did exist, strict rules applied. For instance, in some places gardening was prohibited on weekdays between six a.m. and six p.m. and all day Sunday!

Laws were passed in 1845 to legally secure cheap and accessible allotments. Although the motives were arguably to keep the working classes out of the pub when not slogging away for someone else, this was a momentous change. Allotments of a practical size for purpose became established and popular, especially in urban areas.

In 1919 and 1945, immediately following the two World Wars, well over a million allotments were actively in service. The radical societal and land-use changes since then have seen much leisure garden space lost to development schemes and disuse, but statutory regulations demand that authorities provide these areas for use by the council tax-paying public. Modern sites are havens for people of all races, ages, genders, political persuasions and classes, individuals who seek solace in the company of the soil and what it can produce.

Enthusiasm for allotment gardening comes and goes like most fads and fashions. The first thing to do if the prospect takes your fancy is to visit the local council offices, enquire, and (more than likely) put your name on a waiting list. Depending on the mood of the day, an opportunity to get deep down and dirty may come along sooner than you think. Be prepared!

JANUARY WEEK 2
JOBS TO DO THIS WEEK

IN THE GREENHOUSE
● Keep night cold at bay by covering a lighted candle with a clay pot and letting it burn during the hours of darkness.

ON THE PLOT
● Hand weed around celeriac.
● Hand weed around kale.
● Pay allotment fees to the local council.

JANUARY Week 2: PLANTING APPLE TREES

1. Apples on M26 rootstock are perfect for a small garden. They arrive as one year old 'maiden whips'. Roots are swaddled in plastic or sacking to keep them moist between commercial nursery and private plot.

2. Choose a reasonably sunny, well-drained site. To plant, lever a slot open with a spade. Unwrap the roots. Spread them down deep into the crack with your fingers.

3. Take great care to ensure that the soil mark on the stem (indicated) coincides with the soil level after the slot is firmly but carefully closed around the roots. Air pockets must be avoided or else the tree will suffer.

4. Fit protection around the stem to protect from voles, rabbits and deer. Maintain weed-free soil by placing a mulch-mat around the base. Stake only on exposed sites: facing prevailing winds, drive in a post angled away from the roots. Secure with an adjustable tree-tie.

Having been into town and done the deal I was quite content to ease into a comfy chair for half an hour by the fire with my books and dreams, waiting for swirling raucous winds and accompanying sheets of persistent rain to subside slightly before venturing out into the breach once more.

January   WEEK 3

Preparing Rough Ground

This is an ideal time for preparing a derelict portion of ground for spring planting. It is right to say that transforming weed-infested rough grassland into a clean bed of workable soil can be one of the most physically demanding aspects of home production, but such work offers a chance to build up an intimate and personal relationship with the land. There are no easy ways to do it even with recourse to the dreaded weed killers (which need repeated applications and only do half the job anyway), but a foundation built on honest effort, sweat, and time-devoted, bodes well for many future years of happy gardening.

To begin with, I suggest employing a sturdy rake to drag through the thick weeds and grasses on top. Do this in strips across the plot working backwards, only raking ('scarifying') as much as you plan to clear in that particular session. This teases out most of the dead stuff (of which there is plenty at this time of year), and does a good job of opening up the sward so you can see what you're dealing with.

Ground which hasn't been worked for two years or more will often be a jungle of invasive, wiry white couch-grass and perennial weeds. These must all be completely removed as even small portions of root will survive and cause problems at a later date. The surface debris, also known as 'thatch', is like wet hay. I'd stick it in plastic bags and close the tops with string tied tight. Then stash the bulging bags around the back somewhere for twelve months or so until the contents have rotted down into a crumbly medium. Don't put it on the compost heap. Burning is also an option as it will be full of weed seeds.

Then use a garden fork and toil methodically. Work along the scarified rows. Insert the tines to their full depth with the aid of a boot and lever the handle first forward and then back. This has the effect of tearing the matted vegetation on top then doing likewise with the tangle of roots down below. By pulling the fork up halfway, sods can be lifted up one by one and loose earth shaken free.

Some bits are more co-operative than others. Where the fleshy roots of weeds such as dock, dandelion or hogweed have become well established, more effort and further digging with a spade may be required before the woody impostors can be tugged free with both hands as low down as possible. Others might retain great clods of soil, which is the gardeners' raw material and must be treasured. In this case, gentle knocking with a spare hand or tool handle often proves helpful. Heap the remaining unwanted material in a corner. When the job is done cover with old carpets and leave it to decompose over the next couple of years.

A newly-cleaned patch will contain an enormous bank of weed and grass seeds. Disturbance prompts many of these into germination and it won't be long before the dark earth is tinged with a green haze. This could easily be hoed off in dry weather but such tactics are of no use in the cold and damp of late winter. Instead, place old carpet or sheets of black plastic over the soil as it is cleared. This will keep the persistent weeds at bay until you want to create seed beds and start sowing veggies direct outside in two or three months' time.

Such daunting chores are best tackled bit by bit. Walking away when one is still up for doing more is a good way to motivate for the next visit. An experienced gardener friend of mine hit the nail on the head when he wisely said that thirty minutes here and half an hour there is enough to keep a veg patch ticking over. This good advice is worth taking on board. It is true!

I'm never tempted to use a rotavator either, as these machines merely chop couch and other menaces into little pieces which makes for more work in the long run. If there is no hurry to complete the labours then a thick, light-excluding black plastic sheet laid on top and weighted down with stones or half-bricks will help. Applied thus, this artificial mulch will render the wilderness far easier to tame in over twelve months' time.

JANUARY Week 3: COBNUTS

1. Catkins, which are the male flowers, festoon cobnuts and filberts by mid-January. As they open and elongate catkins resemble lambs' tails. In a breeze puffs of pollen are released and carried in the air.

2. Female flowers are minute red stars borne at the tips of fat buds. When they receive the pollen pollenation and then fertilisation occurs.

3. Bumper crops of plump nuts ripen in late summer and autumn. They must be cracked open to get at the succulent kernel. Filbert husks completely envelop the nut, hence their alternative name of 'full-beard'.

4. Cultivated and wild hazel also make excellent stock-proof hedges. By-products of regular management include walking sticks, bean poles and pea sticks.

JANUARY WEEK 3
JOBS TO DO THIS WEEK

IN THE GREENHOUSE
- Sow Feltham First early peas in pots.
- Sow Tom Thumb lettuce seeds in trays.
- Water seedlings.
- Keep gutters and fixings in good working order.
- Keep threatening night frost at bay with clay pots and candles.

ON THE PLOT
- Check over all areas.
- Continue harvesting winter veg.
- Weed amongst leek bed.
- Tidy lines of swedes.
- Remove outside leaves from leaf beet.
- Clear and dig over a sunny, south-facing bed for early crops to be planted in the near future.
- Remove couch grass from comfrey bed while the latter has completely died down and the wiry underground stems can be easily extracted.

January

Aubergine (Eggplant)

If a little heat is available indoors this is a good time to sow some aubergine seeds. Also known as 'eggplant', this is a highly attractive edible species heralding from warm Eastern and Mediterranean climes. Long Purple is a reliable and traditional variety although there are many different ones to choose from. Pink, frilly, ornamental blooms precede the formation of the elongated oval fruits which swell and dangle like deep purple teardrops, shiny and fascinating. They should be carefully snipped free at harvest time whilst still glossy. At this point they will be a delicious ingredient in all sorts of dishes, or simply thinly sliced and flash-fried in olive oil with a pinch of salt.

With such culinary delights in mind, prepare a seed tray with suitable loam-based compost. Level the medium with a flat firming board and use the end of a nail as a dibber to make little indentations barely 3mm deep at 5cm intervals. The seeds are pinhead-sized, heart-shaped browny-orange disks, and best handled with the aid of tweezers. Empty a scattering in the palm of one hand. Use the tweezers to select the biggest and best looking for sowing, one per indentation. When the tray is full draw a covering of compost over with your dibber and firm ever so gently once more. Watering must be done with a light touch using a small can, thumb half over the spout hole to control the flow to a soft trickle in order not to disturb seeds that are close to the surface.

Alas, I'm not blessed with access to a heated greenhouse, so my charges come into the home and are nurtured on a sunny windowsill with a pane of glass covering the tray until seedlings are showing. Once large enough to handle, I'll prick out (delicately transplant) into 8cm pots and grow them on in the warmth of the porch until mid-April. From here, they will be finally rested in large pots or grow bags, and given pride of place in the greenhouse (now perfect, temperature-wise) alongside tomatoes and okra.

Aubergines can also succeed outdoors if a sunny, sheltered spot is available and the summer is a good one. You'll probably get the most satisfactory returns if you limit your plants to just four fruits each (pick off any others while still tiny). They are ripe for picking from late July until September, with luck. It is important to get them into the kitchen before their vibrant sheen has turned to a dull matt colour. Once this happens, egg plants are beyond their best.

Snowdrops

Mrs Nails' snowdrops are looking particularly fine this year, nodding their plump white heads in praise of the coming spring. Now is the preferred season for planting bunches of these virginal beauties 'in the green'. Popping in clumps of ten at a time with leaves and flowers in full flush is a great way of keeping track of where these spring bulbs have gone.

It is an easy and fun job. Having secured and divided up a supply of snowies from your own garden, the market or garden centre (never from the wild), use a trowel to part the soil as desired. The pretty flowers are tucked in snugly, not too shallow and not too deep. Transformation is instantaneous, delightful, and promises to only get better as the years pass.

Rooks

High aloft in neighbouring woodland this week the handsome figures of rooks shone glossy-black in the bright late winter sunshine. Paired off already, they decorated the uppermost branches of this distinctly English scene with dignity and patience, as they have done for countless generations. A little over a month or so from now, the woods will be a frenzy of organised chaos with the breeding season in full swing. For now, however, the birds seemed to be enjoying a relaxation of the winds, sitting in mellow contemplation of their time to come.

I've always had a soft spot for these communally living members of the crow family. My childhood was spent in the country south of Oxford playing in a garden that was directly beneath a daily, morning and evening, flight path. To and fro the rooks would pass, between their roost and breeding woods (called a rookery) and nearby pastures.

Rooks have distinctive, dagger-like beaks and naked, pale faces, the perfect adaptations for delving deep into farmland soils in search of insect grubs such as leatherjackets and wireworms. Their taste for agricultural grains means that to some they are considered a pest. I have to say that I think the damage done to farmers' interests is negligible and, as far as I am concerned, these friendly birds should be celebrated. The good they do in maintaining the balance of nature is just a bonus when they are in the area.

JANUARY WEEK 4
JOBS TO DO THIS WEEK

IN THE GREENHOUSE
- Check over.
- Ventilate on fine, sunny mornings.
- Sow a tray of Long Black aubergine (take it into the house to germinate unless artificial heat can be provided by a propagator).
- Set out seed potatoes in trays or egg boxes to pre-sprout (chit).

ON THE PLOT
- Hand weed on open ground.
- Prune Beurre Hardy pear grown as a 'bush'.
- Tidy in the shed and make space for spring.
- Check over stored produce, discarding any which is showing signs of going off.

JANUARY Week 4: CHITTING POTATOES

1. Spuds are usually available in the shops by mid-January. This important vegetable is susceptible to a variety of ailments so always purchase certified Disease-Free stock every year.

2. The 'eyes' on a spud show where shoots ('chits') will develop. Set them out in egg-boxes or trays and position in a light, frost-free place to encourage sprouting. Many gardeners believe this helps the crop to mature earlier.

3. 'Blight' is a devastating disease which frequently strikes during hot and humid July. Browning of leaf tips with a ring of white fungal fluff underneath are tell-tale. It can destroy the harvest. Spray copper-based fungicide as a precaution or remove foliage as soon as symptoms are spotted.

4. First Early spuds mature in June for immediate use as 'new potatoes', Second Earlies a month or so later. They will keep until December. Maincrop spuds may be dug from the end of summer. Keep in cool dark, rodent-free conditions for consumption well beyond New Year.

159

January week5

Thinking about Bird Boxes

It may still be early in the year, but you'd be forgiven for thinking that it was much later judging from the twitters of excitement and flutterings of activity in the steep wooded slope behind my back garden wall in the hour after daybreak each morning this week. Amorous blackbirds are playing kiss-chase in the elders, tits and finches flit in pairs and threes or fours, bobbing about from twig to twig then up again, down, across, around.

Thrush, fabulous songster that he is, has cleared his pipes and treats the neighbourhood to a virtuoso performance. His is a rich and exquisite foil to the woodpigeons' familiar, lazy, wheezy, monotonous repeat and woodpeckers' intermittent drilling high from amongst the beeches on top. The breeding season for many garden birds is just about to get into full swing and, with love in the air, now is a good time to put up nest boxes for them. Time is of the essence as the most prolific users of such artificial sites, blue and great tits, are already investigating suitable places in which to raise their broods.

Bearing in mind the fact that tits are fiercely territorial little fellows (unlike sparrows, who like to nest communally), I've positioned a couple of purpose-built nest boxes, one at either end of the plot, securely fixed above the two-metre mark. They are made from a woodchip and concrete mix which is long lasting, easy to clean (with boiling water in the autumn) and also maintains a fairly constant temperature inside. This is an important consideration for the future egg and chick inhabitants, aided by thoughtful siting. Although one box faces north and the other south, both are sheltered from direct sunlight and prevailing weather. They are popular with the birds year after year.

Secure boxes with internal dimensions of about 25cm by 15cm are a good idea, with an entrance hole tailored to fit the species desired. 25mm across will play host to three tits: coal, marsh and blue. 32mm gives access to sparrows and handsome nuthatches, while a hole sized between those two is perfect for great tits. An open-fronted box of similar proportions nestled in amongst, but not obstructed by, thorns or honeysuckle might attract robins, wrens or pied wagtails.

The biggest risk to garden birds, as far as I can make out, is our dangerously high local cat population. My own little puss is knocking on the door of 17. Nowadays, though still in the most beautiful condition and sweet as cherry-pie, she is a wee bit wobbly and delicate at the best of times. For this little queen, hunting days are long gone, but in her prime she was a natural-born killer like the rest. Her worst moment, some years back now, was to wait for Mrs Jenny Wren to raise a brood to fledgling status in a wall cavity below the bathroom window. On the day of their maiden flight she pounced and, one after the other, the family was devastated. I was away at the time working so she laid the haul out in a line by the back door as a present for Mrs Nails.

Poorly-sited nests are irresistible to cats. Not much can be done about them, except to give the birds every chance of success. For instance, a perch at the entrance hole is an unnecessary extra which birds don't need. They only help cats (and squirrels) to gain access. It is the same with overhanging branches, which should be avoided or removed. However, be mindful to make sure that perches are accessible in the vicinity so that when the youngsters leave the nest for the first time they have somewhere safe to get to, be fed grubs by their parents, and take in the big wide world around them. Such perches need to be lightweight and held aloft, unable to support the weight of a cat or other predator. The outermost twiggy branches of an apple tree are ideal.

Local birds will be checking out all these features (and more) in the coming month, before selecting where to settle and feather their nests. The value of a little help from the wildlife-friendly plot holder should not be underestimated. Our domestic gardens account for more land area than all British nature reserves combined. The mix of habitats and trees contained within are crucial to the survival of many species.

JANUARY WEEK 5
JOBS TO DO THIS WEEK

IN THE GREENHOUSE
- Keep door hinges in good repair. Replace or keep well oiled.
- Sow one tray each of leeks, Roxton F1 and Carentan.
- Ventilate on fine mornings.
- Sow Baby Leaf Mixed lettuces.

ON THE PLOT
- Potter and mosey around the plot.
- Plant out winter purslane (which has been nurtured in the greenhouse then hardened-off) around step-over apples.
- Do the same with corn salad plants.
- Dig remaining Jerusalem artichokes and put into store.
- Plant Jerusalem artichoke Fuseau in prepared ground.

JANUARY Week 5: HEELING-IN LEEKS

1. Staple winter crops like leeks can stand until March and occupy ground needed for the next generation of crops. Moving them to a different location, perhaps nearer the kitchen, is no problem.

2. Lift leeks by inserting a fork underneath and levering upwards. Pull gently. Keep as much soil as possible around the mop of white roots.

3. Wheelbarrow or otherwise transport the leeks to the new position. Dig a trench one 'spit' (a spade head) deep in the vacant soil.

4. Place the leeks tightly together in the trench. Pack soil down around the roots and creamy stems. 'Heeled-in' thus, they will stand happily and conveniently for many weeks.

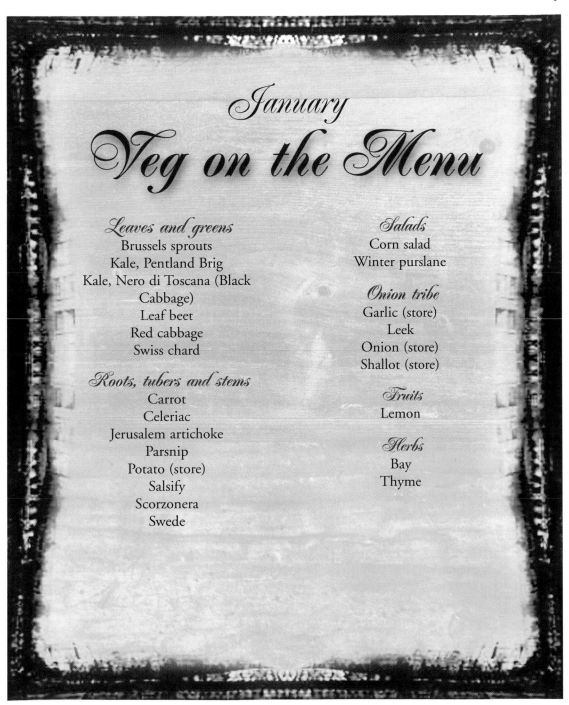

January
Veg on the Menu

Leaves and greens
Brussels sprouts
Kale, Pentland Brig
Kale, Nero di Toscana (Black
    Cabbage)
Leaf beet
Red cabbage
Swiss chard

Roots, tubers and stems
Carrot
Celeriac
Jerusalem artichoke
Parsnip
Potato (store)
Salsify
Scorzonera
Swede

Salads
Corn salad
Winter purslane

Onion tribe
Garlic (store)
Leek
Onion (store)
Shallot (store)

Fruits
Lemon

Herbs
Bay
Thyme

Veg on the Menu

Cabbage Salad

Ingredients
1 teaspoon vinegar
1 teaspoon lemon juice
1 green chilli cut lengthwise (remove before serving)
1 small cabbage, chopped into very tiny pieces
2 teaspoons oil
2 teaspoons mustard seeds

Method
1. Marinate the vinegar, lemon juice and chilli for 10 minutes.
2. Mix the marinade with chopped cabbage, tossing well until all the pieces are covered.
3. In a tiny saucepan heat oil. Then add mustard seeds and fry until they pop. Whilst still hot, pour this mixture over the cabbage and toss again before serving immediately.

Cucumber & Fennel Salad

Ingredients
1 good sized bulb fennel
1 medium cucumber
1 large tomato
Salt & pepper
Juice of half a lime
Drop of olive oil

Method
1. Dice all veg.
2. Toss together with seasoning, oil and juice.
3. Serve when ready.

Simple Fennel Salad

Ingredients
3 or 4 small bulbs of fennel, topped, tailed, cleaned and sliced
A few good squeezes of lemon juice to taste
Salt & pepper
Drizzle of olive oil to taste
1 clove of garlic, thinly sliced

Method
1. Mix all ingredients together and that's it.

Mrs Nails' Potato Salad

Ingredients
Portion of potatoes, amount to suit
Salad dressing (balsamic vinegar, olive oil, lemon, garlic, herbs, sugar)
Salt and pepper
Spoonful of mustard to taste

Method
1. Boil the potatoes, drain and allow to cool.
2. Toss all other ingredients with the potatoes and serve.

Potato and Pea Salad

See July week 2.

Globe Artichoke Dip

Ingredients
4 fist-sized globe artichokes
2 tablespoons olive oil
1 clove garlic
Juice of 1 lemon or lime
Twist of salt & pepper

Method
1. Prepare the artichokes by boiling until tender. Scrape the flesh from each 'leaf' and save. Avoid the choke. Separate the 'hearts' out for roasting separately.
2. Mix and mash all the combined ingredients together, then whizz with a hand blender.
3. Serve with sweet baby carrots, cucumber cut into sticks, potato chips or simply spread onto hot toast. De-licious!

Vegetable Risotto

Ingredients
1 large onion, chopped
350g rice
1.1 litres of stock
Mug full of peas
Seasoning to taste
Olive oil for frying

Method
1. Fry the onion gently in olive oil till well coated.
2. Add the rice and mix well.
3. Make up the vegetable stock and gradually add to pan as it gets absorbed.
4. Add peas and keep stirring well. Season well.

Optional extra: Cheese or cheese substitute may be grated over when served.

Stuffed Peppers

Ingredients
4 red peppers
4 spring onions
10 cherry tomatoes
1 garlic clove
250g boiled rice
Large can baked beans
Small can kidney beans
Chopped parsley
Seasoning

Method
1. Preheat oven to 200C/gas mark 6.
2. Halve and de-seed peppers. Place skin side down on a baking sheet.
3. Chop spring onions, quarter the tomatoes and crush the garlic.
4. Place in bowl with the cooked rice, beans, shopped parsley and seasoning and mix very well.
5. Divide the mixture between the pepper halves and bake for 25–30 minutes.
6. Serve hot with mixed salad.

Spinach Puree

Ingredients
2 huge handfuls of spinach washed, chopped and ready to eat (it will reduce to almost nothing)
1 decent-sized onion, diced
4 or 5 mushrooms, sliced
Drop of oil
Salt to taste
Method
1. Cook the spinach in as little water as possible to retain maximum goodness.
2. Puree the cooked spinach with a hand blender and add salt as required.
3. Fry onion and mushrooms in oil.
4. When they have nicely softened and 'sweated' add the spinach and serve.

Cinzia's Pomodori Con il Riso (Tomatoes Stuffed with Rice)

This is a classic summer Roman dish that is delicious eaten either hot or cold. In the Roman recipe the stuffed tomatoes are cooked with potatoes or you can enjoy them on their own.

For best results it is crucial to use sun-ripened large (beef tomatoes) and freshly picked herbs.

Ingredients
4 large tomatoes (1 tomato per person) or eight small ones
4 tablespoons of Arborio rice (1-1½ tablespoons for each tomato depending on size)
1 handful of fresh chopped basil
1 handful of fresh chopped mint
1 handful of fresh chopped oregano (optional)
1 handful of fresh chopped thyme (optional)
2 garlic cloves, chopped
Coarse salt
Olive oil
Potatoes (4 large)
Salt & pepper to taste

Method

1. Slice the caps off the tomatoes and set aside.
2. Use a spoon and scoop out seed and pulp of the tomatoes. Carefully transfer them to a bowl.
3. Be careful not to tear the skin.
4. Sprinkle the insides of the tomatoes' shells with coarse salt.
5. Add some olive oil (2 tablespoons), salt and pepper to the tomatoes' pulp and seeds placed in the bowl.
6. Stir and add the rice, the chopped mint, basil and garlic. Stir well and set aside for at least an hour.
7. Preheat the oven to 180C/gas mark 4.
8. Peel the potatoes, cut them in quarters length-wise.
9. Fill the tomatoes with the rice mixture.
10. Replace the caps on the tomatoes and arrange them in a baking dish. Put the potatoes wedges amongst them.
11. Pour the remaining tomato juice and oil all over (add further olive oil if needed).
12. Bake for at least an hour, basting the tomatoes and the potatoes frequently with the juices in the dish.
13. Serve the tomatoes and potatoes together.

'Buon appetito!'

Hannah's Borsch

Ingredients
6 beetroot (or more)
3 medium potatoes
1 small onion, chopped
2 medium carrots, grated
Kale or medium-sized cabbage, shredded (2 handfuls, add more or less to taste)
3 or 4 sticks celery
3 tablespoons flat-leaved parsley, chopped
1 tablespoon garlic, minced
2 bay leaves
2 teaspoons dill seeds
2 teaspoons oregano
3 tablespoons tomato paste
3 tablespoons red wine vinegar
1 vegetable stock cube
Approximately 1.5 litres of water
Salt & pepper to taste
Sugar to taste
To garnish: (soya) cream, fresh dill

Method
1. Before everything, roast beets whole in the oven with their skins on.
2. Sauté onions, celery and grated carrot until soft.
3. Add garlic, oregano, dill, bay leaves. Cook for 1 minute.
4. Add red wine vinegar and glaze the pan by sloshing it around to coat the herbs and pan sides.
5. Add water, stock, salt, pepper. Bring to the boil then turn down to simmer.
6. Meanwhile, take beets from the oven and slip them from their skins. Grate or shred finely when cool.
7. Add beets, chopped potatoes, shredded kale or cabbage, parsley and tomato paste.
8. Simmer and stir on a low heat for 30 minutes (or until the potatoes are cooked) then serve.

Hannah's top tip: step 6 is a very messy job. If you don't fancy staining your hands red then wear gloves.

Carrot & Courgette Soup

Ingredients

110g margarine
450g carrots
450g courgettes
550ml vegetable stock,
2 tablespoons tomato puree
1 tablespoons sugar (optional)
2 bay leaves
Seasoning to taste

Method

1. Peel carrots and slice. Top and tail courgettes and slice (leave skin on).
2. Melt margarine in saucepan, add veg and cook until soft.
3. Add other ingredients and simmer gently for about 15 minutes.
4. Remove bay leaves, liquidise in blender and serve.

Butternut Squash & Carrot Soup

Ingredients

1 large squash
4 large carrots
1 medium onion
Olive oil
Bay leaf
Vegetable stock
Seasoning to taste

Method

It is easier if you halve the squash, scoop out seeds and bake in the oven until soft – that way you can scrape out the squash and leave the skin.
1. Fry the onion in olive oil till soft, then add the cut carrots, stock, bay leaf and seasoning and bring to boil.
2. Add the squash and let it all simmer until the carrots are cooked and then blend.

Chilli Kale Soup

Ingredients
2 medium parsnips
½ large squash
3 small (or 1 large) potatoes
3 small (or 1 large) leeks
6 Jerusalem artichokes
Kale, as much as you like (it will reduce drastically in cooking)
1 small red chilli
Lemon juice
Vegetable stock cube
Oil
1.6 litres water

Method
1. Hot fry the Jerusalems (with a splash of lemon juice added to the oil) in the pot until really brown and soft.
2. Add leeks sliced lengthways, diced squash, parsnips and spuds. Fry off with chilli until all slightly brown and sizzling.
3. Add 1 litre of water and simmer for half an hour.
4. Add kale and another 600ml of water. Simmer another half hour.
5. Blend roughly with a hand whizzer and serve hot with hunks of bread.

Mrs Nails' Leek & Potato Soup

Ingredients
4 medium potatoes
4 Leeks
Mug of peas
1 onion
Handful of greens (such as turnip tops, sprig of celery, leaf beet)
2 tablespoons wholegrain mustard
Vegetable stock
Knob margarine
(Soya) milk
Salt and ground pepper (to taste)

Method
1. Sauté the onion in margarine until soft.
2. Add diced potatoes, leeks, peas and greens.
3. Sauté for a further 5 to 10 minutes.
4. Add vegetable stock and (soya) milk half and half to cover the vegetables.
5. Add mustard.
6. Simmer gently for approximately half an hour until the potatoes are soft.
7. Liquidize with a hand blender and serve.

Derek's Nettle Soup

See May week 1

Summer Soup

Ingredients

Summer veg, amount and combination to suit (e.g. red and white onions, broad beans, peas, carrots, spuds, thinly sliced fennel, baby leaves of lettuces and 'greens')
2 or 3 good sprigs of each of parsley and mint
Vegetable stock
Pepper
Olive oil

Method

1. Sauté onions.
2. Add chopped veg and sauté further.
3. Make up enough stock to generously cover all the vegetables.
4. Add baby leaves and half the herbs. Bring to the boil then simmer until cooked.
5. Just before serving, chop up and stir in remaining herbs and pepper to taste.

Spicy Winter Soup

Ingredients
1 large thumb of ginger
1 tin of coconut milk
3 or 4 garlic cloves
6 or 7 shallots
2 medium leeks
1 large celeriac
1 small parsnip
1 small swede
4 big potatoes
2 handfuls of frozen peas
1 good bunch of kale
Juice from one ripe lime
2 teaspoons vegetable bouillon
Fresh chilli to taste
Salt & pepper to taste

Method
1. Heat oil.
2. Add chopped shallots and leeks, garlic, chilli and ginger. Toss and fry until translucent and soft.
3. Add all the other chopped-up veg except peas and kale.
4. Splash in the coconut milk and vegetable bouillon to cover the ingredients by about an inch (2.5cm).
5. Bring to the boil then throw in the peas.
6. Simmer until almost cooked (test pieces of potato to check).
7. Add the kale 10 minutes from the end (turn the heat off if needs be).
8. Roughly pureé with a hand blender. If consistency is too thick just add some more veg boullion.
9. Season to taste with salt and pepper. If it's not spicy enough at this stage simply stir in extra finely diced chilli complete with the seeds.

Mrs E's Spicy Sweet Potato Soup

'This is my recipe for a lovely, warming, hearty soup. I made this at home and Joshua kept on nagging me to make it for the boys at school. I wasn't sure they would like it because 99% of them come from Ashkanasi (Polish/Russian backgrounds) and this is more of a Sephardi (Middle Eastern) recipe. It became an instant hit and there is great disappointment if I ever miss a week of not making it.

'The amounts are very approximate - it really depends on how hot and spicy you like it.'

Ingredients
2 large sweet potatoes, peeled and cut into chunks
1 tablespoon olive oil
1 teaspoon paprika
1 teaspoon ground cumin
½ teaspoon chilli powder
Chopped garlic 2 cloves garlic, chopped
1 teaspoon harissa (chilli paste) or red chilli chopped
Vegetable stock - enough to cover the potatoes, plus a bit more
Ground black pepper
Salt, if needed

Method
1. Gently fry all the spices in heated oil for couple of minutes.
2. Add sweet potatoes and 'sweat' for a minute or two.
3. Add veg stock. Bring to boil and simmer until soft.
4. Blend soup. Add extra water and seasoning if needed.
5. Serve with huge chunks of bread and enjoy!

Mrs E's top tip: 'If you really want to show off, you can serve it in bowls made from bread. Bread, similar to pizza dough, rolled out in circles and put over greased ovenproof dishes. Brushed with olive oil and baked for about 20 minutes. VERY impressive!'

Watercress Soup

Ingredients
3 bunches watercress
225ml stock
225ml water
25g margarine
1 large chopped onion and potato

Method
1. Melt marge and cook onion and potato for approximately 5 minutes, then add the water and simmer for 15 minutes.
2. Cut stems from watercress, add to pan with the stock and just bring to boil just for a minute. Season and cool.
3. Blend all.

Optional extra: Cream may be added if you wish.

Potatoes & Tomatoes in Gravy

Ingredients
4 potatoes, pre-boiled in reasonably large chunks
2 tablespoons oil
1 tablespoon cumin seeds
1 small thumb of fresh ginger, grated
1green chilli, chopped
½ teaspoon haldi
1 onion, chopped
2 tomatoes, chopped
1 teaspoon dhaniya powder
½ teaspoon chilli powder
Salt to taste
Water as required to prevent burning
1 teaspoon kala masala

Method
1. Fry cumin seeds. Add chilli powder and haldi when oil is hot. If a choking (but not burning) smoke is given off this is a good sign as it means the spices are cooking as they should.
2. Add all the other ingredients at this stage except the tomatoes, potatoes and kala masala. Bring to the boil.
3. Add tomatoes and potatoes then simmer for 25 minutes.
4. When cooked, add kala masala and stir it in just before serving. If you add this spice earlier then it loses all its flavour so sprinkle in at the very end.

Stuffed Brinjal

Ingredients
1 whole aubergine (aka brinjal)
Stuffing ingredients (mix together before cooking):
2 onions, grated
Lots of garlic (grated/chopped/sliced very fine)
Salt to taste
1 or 2 teaspoons fennel seeds
2 or 3 teaspoons dhaniya

Method
1. Slit the aubergine along its length every 4 or 5cm; just cut slits so that each one can be opened a little, not so much that you end up cutting all the way through.
2. Press the stuffing mix into each opening.
3. Fry on a low heat until cooked. The aubergine flesh will be soft at this point and the stuffing should have gone soggy and be kind of diminished. It is best to do this with a lid on the pan to ensure thorough all round cooking of the aubergine.
4. When ready, garnish with boiled potatoes which are cut into lengths and put in the slits.
5. Sprinkle over the top with dhaniya (again) and serve.

Methi & Potato Bhugia

Ingredients
Oil
¼ teaspoon mustard seeds
½ teaspoon haldi
½ teaspoon chilli powder
Salt to taste
1 teaspoon dhaniya
1 heaped teaspoon methi (dried)
1 teaspoon garam masala
4 medium-sized potatoes, chopped

Method
1. Heat oil, fry mustard seeds until they pop then quickly add chilli powder and haldi. An acrid smell from the pan is a good sign that the spices are cooking authentically.
2. Add dhaniya, salt and chopped potatoes, stir, sprinkle methi all over and stir again. Cover and steam or fry over a low heat.
3. When the potatoes are tender add garam masala and fry hard for 1 or 2 minutes.

Variation: you could add cauliflower florets as well as the spuds.

Peppers Bhugia

Ingredients
Oil
¼ teaspoon mustard seeds
½ teaspoon chilli powder
½ teaspoon haldi
1 teaspoon dhaniya
Salt to taste
2 green peppers (or green/yellow, green/red, any combination is okay), sliced/chopped

Method
1. Heat oil. When hot add mustard seeds which will pop noisily and often right out of the pan. As they are popping add chilli powder and haldi. Await that acrid smell which comes almost immediately. Watch out that the oil does not get so hot that the spices actually burn.
2. Add peppers, dhaniya and salt, stir well and cover. Fry on a low heat until cooked.
3. Serve!

Hot Onions, Fennel and Cabbage

Ingredients
1 good-sized red onion
2 bulbs of Florence fennel
Thick head of summer cabbage
Salt & pepper
Olive oil

Method
1. Heat a little oil in pan.
2. Add salt and pepper when hot (pepper should sizzle).
3. Add veggies, sliced and diced.
4. Mix with a spatula.
5. Put lid on pan and turn off electric to cook on residual heat (if gas: put lid on pan and cook on lowest flame possible) for 20 minutes. Stir occasionally.
6. Serve with boiled spuds and pies.

Stuffed Cabbage

Ingredients
Any large leaf cabbage
175g rice
1 large onion, grated
275ml stock
2 tablespoon tomato puree
25 g sugar
2 tablespoons lemon juice
Seasoning
450g mince or veggies substitute (Quorn, textured soya protein, etc)

Tip: If using Dutch cabbage, place in freezer overnight and the leaves will peel off easily.
Otherwise soak cabbage in boiling water.

Method
1. Drain and dry cabbage leaves, cutting away any hard stalks.
2. Mix mince/substitute, rice, onion and a tablespoon of puree, lemon juice and seasoning.
3. Place a spoonful of mixture into each leaf and roll up – pack these tightly into large casserole dish with the stock. Mix remaining puree, sugar and lemon juice and pour over cabbage (if needed, add a little more stock).
4. Cover and cook at 150C/gas mark 2 for about 2½-3 hours.

Crapple Jelly

This delicious amber jelly recipe was a favourite of Edward (Max) Pearson, former head gardener at the American Museum near Bath. He was a great grower of fruit and veg and loved making jams and jellies.
It is perfect on toast or bread, can be used to make sauces or for glazing cakes or to sweeten puddings and desserts.

1. Gather a bag full of crab apples, both windfalls and picked, preferably the orangey-red ones such as John Downie. Halve them, discarding the really rotten bits, and shove in a saucepan with water to cover by half an inch.
2. Boil until soft and allow to cool. Pour the lot into a muslin cloth and tie it up so that it can strain into a large bowl overnight.
3. For each pint of juice you collect, allow 450g of sugar. Stir the juice and sugar in a large pan over a low heat until dissolved, then turn up the heat.
4. Meanwhile, place clean dry jam jars (not the lids) onto a baking tray and put into a warmish oven.
4. As the mixture boils, skim off any scum on the top. Place 3-4 small saucers in the fridge.
5. Once it reaches a rolling boil, after about 25 minutes, begin to test whether it is ready: dip a wooden spoon into the mixture, then allow it to drip off the edge of the spoon. If the drips start to join up so that it hangs in curtains, it is ready. Alternatively, drip a teaspoonful onto a cold saucer, pop it back in the fridge for a couple of minutes and then push the surface of the jelly with your finger. If it wrinkles, it's ready.
6. Bring the jars out of the oven and fill, using a jug and/or ladle. Cover and seal.

Variations: at stage 1, try adding sliced raw root of ginger, or a stick of cinnamon.
Note: The strained juice will freeze perfectly well if you are not ready to make the jelly straight away.

Chocolate Strawberry Cake

Ingredients

Cake mix (dry)
240g self-raising flour
250g sugar
3 tablespoons unsweetened cocoa
2¼ teaspoons bicarbonate of soda
1 teaspoon egg replacement
pinch of salt

Cake mix (wet)
225ml chocolate (soya) milk
100ml sunflower oil
3 teaspoons cider vinegar
Vanilla essence, a few drops

Filling
Strawberry jam
Fresh sliced strawberries
Swirl (soya) cream

Topping
Icing sugar
Cocoa
Walnut pieces
Grated chocolate

Method
1. Pre-heat oven to 150C/gas mark 2.
2. Grease and line 2 sandwich sponge cake tins.
3. Mix wet cake mix ingredients together in a bowl.
4. Mix dry cake mix ingredients together in another bowl.
5. When oven is hot, add wet to dry and mix together but do not beat. Then smooth contents into cake tins half and half. (Hannah's note: This can look pretty rank when you're putting the ingredients together but trust! It's choc-tastic!)
6. Put into the oven and leave until a skewer can be inserted and pulled out cleanly.
7. Turn out and leave to thoroughly cool before icing.
8. Mix cocoa powder and icing sugar with a drop of water and ice top half of the cake.
9. Put strawberries on top with grated chocolate.
10. Spread jam and strawberry slices on top of the bottom half of the cake.
11. Put the top on the bottom and call your friends to share!

Kate O'Farrel's Blackberry Whisky

'I first tasted rich and smooth blackberry whisky while on holiday in the village of Durness in the far north west of Scotland. Since we have an abundance of blackberries in the wild patches of our community orchard in Shaftesbury, I thought I'd give it a go using the same technique as for sloe gin. The quantities can be adjusted to perfect your own recipe.'

Ingredients
500g blackberries
150g sugar
75cl bottle of whisky

Method
Sterilise a 1.5 litre airtight jar (or equivalent smaller jars) by immersing in boiling water for 10 minutes then dry in a low oven. Sterilise the rubber seals by immersing in boiling water.

Wash the fruit in several changes of water and discard any that persistently float on the surface. Put the fruit and sugar in the jar and top up with whisky. Shake the jars to mix in the sugar and store in a cool dry cupboard. Shake every day until the sugar is completely dissolved, then occasionally to keep things well mixed.

Leave until Christmas or beyond if you can. Strain through muslin or clean cotton into sterilised bottles. If kept for longer you may want to pass through a coffee filter to clear any remaining sediment. It's a great festive drink but if you can save some until the following winter all the better as the flavour will have intensified.

RECIPES FROM LOUISE 'TEDDY' EDWARDS OF 'NIRVANA', POST OFFICE LANE, LIGHTHORNE, WARWICKSHIRE. 27th February 1918 to 27th December 1994.

'It's the stored memories that make death irrelevant. As long as memories are active that person goes on and on and never dies.' John Cox, Shaftesbury, 20th March 2009.

Louise Cox was born Louise Thurlbourne-Edwards in Hockley Heath, Birmingham on February 27th 1918. She became a trained and state-registered nurse but, suffering from glaucoma, was forced to forsake the career path of her choosing at just eighteen years of age.

From 1953 until 1968 'Teddy', as she was affectionately known, relocated to the Warwickshire village of Lighthorne near Leamington Spa with her husband Neville and two sons. Despite having extremely poor eyesight, she was always busy and never idle. She loved both other people and their company. Teddy was a country woman who spent much of her time outdoors in the fields and woods which were so close to her heart. This passion for the natural world survives in the sons whom she doted on, John and Rich.

In those days just after World War Two there was neither the quantity or diversity of foods available in the shops to buy. But living in the country as Teddy did, she recognised the edible potential which still existed for free in the landscape.

Her son John told me, 'It was a different world. Everyone grew vegetables or kept a pig. Everybody had an allotment which was very busy at weekends. And making alcoholic drinks was a way of preserving the wild things that would otherwise be wasted. She could capture the taste (of elderflowers) in the drink. I remember collecting apples. There were so many eventually we'd just shake the trees and they'd fall down and get bruised. But we lined every drawer in the bedrooms with paper and stored the apples until Christmas. The smell! Half went rotten but the other half was okay.

'And salting runner beans! She'd chop them up the same as if they were for eating and put a layer of them in a big jar. Then salt then beans then salt up to the top and then fill it with tap water I think. I remember the absolute sheer joy of having runner beans on Christmas Day. You'd just wash the salt off and they were as good as fresh. Oh, and she had a big copper pan which always seemed to be full of strawberries boiling up for jam. And my grandmother had more plums in her garden than anyone could ever eat! There were still not the insecticides about in those days. But the harvest was so heavy every year we didn't need them. She made her plum jam thinking one jar for the maggots and three jars for me.

'Everything was done in season. What you could eat you ate, what you couldn't you bottled. People were never doing nothing. In the villages there was always something on the go. There was no telly or computers you see, no nothing, so people worked when they were at home except it wasn't really work. It was, I don't know really, it was a way of having the best to eat in or out of season. Everybody was digging, everybody was preserving. Those were the old ways. I was brought up that if you don't use it, whatever it is, it's just going to waste.'

John still treasures the extensive hand-written journals of observations, poetry and recipes which survive from those golden days. It is from these that I have deciphered a selection of his mother's secrets to share with you. Try them if you dare! They are recorded here exactly as she wrote them. Teddy was a great experimenter and John recalls her as always having several brews on the go. 'Everyone in the village was home-brewing,' he recalled fondly.

Dandelion Wine

5 pints dandelion flowers
1 gallon water
3lb sugar
2 oranges
1 lemon

Put in a bag
Boil for 15 minutes
Take flowers out
Put sugar to wine, boil 20 mins
Work with a bit of yeast
Put into jars with a few raisins
Work for a few days.

Wittenham Cider

Mince 1lb cooking apples including peel and cores
Pour on 6 quarts cold unboiled water
Leave for 1 week stirring night and morning
Strain liquid
Stir in 2lb granulated sugar add grated rind and juice of 3 lemons
Set aside for 24 hours and bottle
Ready in one week.

Peach Wine

2lb peaches
1 gallon water
2½ lbs sugar
1 lemon
1 orange

Soak peaches overnight in gallon of water
Boil until tender
Strain off hot liquid
Add sugar and lemon and orange thinly sliced when cool
Add yeast leave 10 days, stirring once a day.

Orange Wine

4 oranges
1 lemon
1 oz ginger
Yeast

Boil water, orange peel and ginger for 1 hour
Pour boiling liquid over sliced oranges and sugar
When cool add yeast
Put in jars for 3 or 4 days.

Apricot Wine

1lb dried apricots
1½ lb white sugar
2 Campden tabs
1 gallon water
Yeast

Cut apricots into small pieces
Pour boiling over them
Add crushed Campden tabs
Stir twice daily for 3 days
Add yeast and leave another week
Strain
Dissolve sugar in liquid and pour into jar.

Damson Wine

4lbs damsons
3lb white sugar
1 gallon water

Wash and drain fruit
Bruise well with wooden spoon
Add boiling water
Leave for 4 days stirring each day
Squeeze through muslin
Add sugar and yeast.

To Pickle Cauliflower

Cut the cauliflower in small pieces - put them in a pan. Pour over them some boiling water, let it stand 24 hours. Then boil the water again and again pour it over and let it stand as before. The third day repeat the process with fresh salt and water - then well drain the cauliflower.

Chillis, white pepper and crushed ginger to taste. Put in vinegar and simmer but be sure not to boil as it will destroy the flavour.

When cool pour over the cauliflower, and cover the bottle with brown paper.

To Pickle Cauliflower- - Another Way

Make some strong salt and water in a saucepan. Let it boil. Drop the pieces of cauliflower in when boiling. Let them boil two minutes - not more or it will become soft. Drain them and pickle them with the vinegar and spice as before.

Metric/Imperial conversions

75cl	½ tablespoon
100ml	3.5 fluid ounces
225 ml	8 fluid ounces
275 ml	½ pint
1.1 litres	2 pints
1.5 litres	2.6 pints
2 pints	1.1 litres
5 pints	2.84 litres
1 gallon	4.5 litres
25 g	1 oz
110 g	4 oz
150 g	5 oz
175 g	6 oz
225 g	8 oz
240 g	8.4 oz
250 g	9 oz
350 g	¾ lb
450 g	1 lb
500 g	1 lb 2 oz
1 oz	28.35 g
1 lb	0.45 kg
2 lb	0.9 kg
3 lb	1.35 kg
150 degrees Celsius	302 degrees Farenheit
200 degrees Celsius	400 degrees Farenheit
2.5 cm	1 inch
15cm	6 inches
30 cm	1 foot
1 metre	3.3 feet

Glossary of Terms

Adventitious shoots: shoots growing in abnormal positions.

Apple and Spoon Race: game played by balancing an apple on a spoon then competing with other people doing likewise in a race.

Apples on Strings: game where apples are suspended from a structure on strings so that they dangle. Players must eat the apples without using their hands.

Aspect: describes the position of a crop in relation to the sun, shelter and prevailing winds.

Base dressing: application of fertilisers or manures to the underground root-zones of veggies, often by digging a trench, flopping in the additive then refilling.

Bare-rooted: mainly refers to trees and shrubs which have been grown in the soil and arrive from nurseries or other gardens immediately after lifting with their roots protected by straw or plastic sacking.

Bastard trenching: *see* Double-digging.

Bedding in: settling of freshly relocated plant into its new growing position.

Biennial: flowers or fruits in the year after sowing.

Blighted: fungal disease, especially affecting potatoes and tomatoes. May also refer to blackfly infestations on beans.

Bobbing Apples: game played where apples are floated in a tub of water and participants must grab and remove them with their mouths only (not hands).

Bolting: when a plant rushes to produce flowers earlier than expected, usually caused by environmental factors such as drought or disturbance.

Brassica: family name for members of the cabbage tribe.

Broadcast sow: to scatter seeds by hand over an area, as opposed to careful sowing in rows.

Bulky organic matter: manure, compost, leafmould.

Bush (apple): apple tree with an open centre branching from the trunk at about 2½ feet (75cm), often grown on an 'M26' rootstock.

Caterpillar: the worm- or maggot-like larva of butterflies and moths.

Chitting (potato): setting out individual potato tubers in a frost-free and light place so shoots may develop before planting.

Choke, as in artichoke: the immature flower petals which cannot be eaten.

Cloche: a clear covering for early and late season veg production which is portable.

Cocoon: a protective envelope secreted by insects in which they can pupate.

Cold frame: a box-like structure usually made of bricks, but can be wood, with glass top ('lights'). Used to nurture early or late crops or as a halfway house for tender veggies between the protected greenhouse environment and open air of the plot.

Companion planting: the act of planting different species together in close proximity for the positive effects they have on each other.

Compost: an organic material made up principally of decomposed vegetable matter.

Container-grown: fruit or veggies raised in pots or tubs.

Coppicing: the act of cutting trees and shrubs to just above ground level, usually on a rotation of several years.

Cover crop: specially grown crop which protects and binds the soil with its leaves and roots.

Cross pollination: transfer of pollen (male) from one plant to the anther (female) of another.

Crown (asparagus): the spider-like roots and underground base of an asparagus plant.

Crown (globe artichoke): base of the plant at ground level or just below.

Cucurbit: family name for cucumbers, squashes, courgettes and marrows.

Dead-head: remove spent flowers to promote further bloom production.

De-leaf: remove leaves.

Dibber: tool used to make holes in prepared soil for planting young veggies.

Direct sowing: sowing seeds straight into a prepared seed bed in the open soil.

Double digging: cultivation technique where the soil is cultivated to the depth of two spade heads.

Double flowered: flower form with more than the normal amount of petals in numerous rows and often lacking in male reproductive organs.

Drill: shallow furrow made in prepared ground in which seeds are sown.

Early Maincrops (pea): varieties sown around early March for cropping in June/July.

Earth up: to draw soil up around the base of a plant. Integral to potato cultivation but also applicable to leeks, celery, carrots and others.

Easterlies: winds that blow in from Continental Europe across the North Sea.

Ecosystem: a defined area containing all the living organisms and non-living material.

Ericaceous compost: growing medium specially formulated for acid-loving plants.

Espalier: Tree trained to have side branches growing opposite each other off a main central stem and maintained by pruning.

Evergreen: plant that keeps its leaves all year round as opposed to shedding them in the autumn or winter.

Eye (potato): the point from which growth sprouts emerge.

First Early (pea): varieties suited for sowing in autumn (to over-winter with protection) or January/February for an extra early harvest in May or June.

First Early (potato): quick maturing variety of potato which is ready to dig in June.

Formative pruning: pruning carried out on young trees to establish a basic framework of branches as desired by the gardener.

Fruiting spur: short, fruit-bearing branch.

Gardener's Shuffle: small sideways steps taken forwards and backwards to firm a bed, principally before the planting of onions or brassicas.

Germinate: term used to describe what happens when a seed starts to sprout.

Green manure: a quick-growing crop grown to replenish nutrients and body in a soil, to protect it, or all of these.

Growing medium: soil or compost.

Harden off: the act of putting young crops from a protected environment outside during late-spring daytime to acclimatise them, but bringing them under cover at night.

Hardy annual: frost resistant plant that completes its lifecycle in one season.

Haulm: the leaves above ground of potatoes or leaves and stems of beans and tomatoes.

Hibernate: to pass winter in a dormant state, for survival purposes.

Hilum: scar on the surface of a seed which shows where it was attached to the seed stalk.

Horticultural fleece: thin sheet of man-made fibre which is used to cover crops as protection from the weather or pests.

Hungry gap: the period between the end of stored and over-wintered veg and the onset of the current season's harvest, usually between late March and early May.

Hybrid: the offspring of genetically different parent plants.

Iceberg: lettuce, also known as 'crisphead lettuce', with dense, round head not unlike a cabbage.

Invertebrate: an animal without a backbone.

Lattice pots: perforated plastic pots which are used to provide root anchorage for underwater pond and marsh plants.

Leafmould: decomposed leaves when they form a fine and crumbly medium.

Leaf node: junction of leaf and stem from where new growth arises.

Liquid feed: fertiliser applied in liquid form, usually diluted with water.

Loam-based compost: proprietary compost with added sterilised garden soil.

Long-handled edging irons: long-handled shears which can be used to trim lawn and path edges without the need to bend down.

Longest Peel: game where competitors try to peel an apple whilst ensuring that the peel comes away in one piece.

Maiden whip: *see* Whip.

Maincrop (potato): varieties of potato ready for harvesting in September or October from a late-spring planting. Also describes varieties of veg which produce the bulk of their crops in the main growing season.

Mulch: protective layer of material placed on top and/or around plants to suppress weeds and conserve water.

Native: plant or animal which occurs naturally within these shores and has not been introduced by people.

On The Plot

Nursery bed: specially prepared and managed area for raising young vegetables between the seedling and planting out stages, especially useful in cultivation of leeks and brassicas.

Pinch out: remove manually with the finger tips.

Pollarding: the act of cutting trees at head height or above to encourage multi-stemmed fresh growth.

Pollen: a fine powdery substance produced by the male flower parts of seed-bearing plants.

Pot-grown: plants which have been grown or raised in containers.

Potting on/potted on: to move plants which have outgrown the size of their pots into larger containers.

Prick out: to carefully remove seedlings from a seed tray into individual pots.

Puddle in: drench the immediate area of the roots and allow soil to settle naturally (principally in leek cultivation).

Pupa: non-feeding stage of insect development between larva and adult.

Root-ball: the knot of roots and growing medium either in the soil or within a pot/container.

Rootstock: part of a grafted plant (usually a fruit tree) which provides the roots.

Root zone: area where the roots are feeding.

Sacrificial crop: plants grown to tempt pests away from more highly prized crop, such as nasturtiums acting as a decoy for cabbages.

Salad (potato): varieties of potato cultivated as Maincrops but developed specifically for eating cold after cooking.

Scab (potato): disease which disfigures the surface of potatoes with rough patches but is only skin deep. Most likely to occur in dry seasons and does not affect eating qualities.

Scrump (scrumping): the act of taking edible produce, often apples and pears but could be veggies as well, without permission from the grower.

Second Early (potato): early maturing varieties ready to dig in July, after the First Earlies but before the Maincrops.

Seed beds: ground specifically prepared to a fine texture for the direct sowing of seeds.

Seed leaves: botanically known as 'cotyledons', these are the first leaves to emerge from the seed immediately following germination.

Seedling: name given to a plant in the early stages of growth.

Self-seed: reproduces itself from seeds sown naturally (without help from the gardener).

Set (onion): immature onions, part-grown and then heat-treated. Can be planted in spring for crops in late summer, or autumn for harvesting the next May/June.

Sett (badger): name used to describe the badgers' subterranean dwelling.

Single-flowered: basic flower form with one row of usually four to six petals.

Spit: in gardening terms, this refers to the length of a spade-head.

Splat the Apple: game played with a cricket bat or similar and windfall apples. Apples are tossed by a 'bowler' to the 'batter' and they try to smash it to smithereens. Often enjoyed by children but adults find it irresistible too.

Spot weed: remove individual weeds as and when they are seen.

Spuds: alternative name for potatoes.

Spur prune (top fruit): on trained espalier trees, summer pruning in late July (August in the North) of laterals (side branches) back to three leaves to promote clusters of fruiting buds on old wood.

Standing crops: mature crops which are still on the plot in the open soil where they were grown.

Station sow: when seeds are sown two or three at a time in a row at regular intervals (e.g. three seeds every 15cm for parsnips).

Stem: The main body of a plant which is usually (but not always) above ground supporting the leaves and branches.

Succession sow: to sow seeds of a vegetable variety a little and often to ensure small supplies coming to fruition over a long period of time rather than a glut of produce all in one go.

Summer prune (top fruit): cut out the current season's woody stems to inhibit growth and channel energy into producing fruit next year.

Swan-necked hoe: also called a 'draw hoe', useful for earthing up around crops or chopping off larger weeds at the root.

Tamp: firm gently with the end of a rake held so it is flat.

Thinning out: the act of reducing the number and density of plants growing in close proximity to each other.

On The Plot

Tie in: the act of tying branches and stems to supporting structures in trained fruit trees and vegetables such as tomatoes and beans.

Tilth: of soil, the fine and crumbly surface created by careful cultivation.

Titmouse: alternative name for members of the tit family of garden birds.

Top dress: to apply a material to the soil surface to replenish body or nutrients.

Top fruit: apples, pears and plums mainly.

Topped 'n' tailed: in beans and carrots, to nick off the extreme ends of the edible portion with a knife or sharp finger nails.

Torpid: apathetic, sluggish or lethargic. How an insect would seem whilst hibernating.

Truss: compact cluster of flowers or fruits.

Ubiquitous: something that seems to have the ability to be everywhere at once.

Under-storey, woodland: also called the 'shrub layer', describes the woody plants which grow beneath the canopies of tall trees but above herbaceous and flowering plants.

Vine eye: metal peg inserted into the masonry between bricks to attach wires for training climbing plants.

Volunteer: potato or Jerusalem artichoke tuber which gets overlooked at harvest time then grows the following season.

Wassail: to bless fruit trees with toast and cider to ward off evil spirits and encourage a bountiful harvest, usually done on Twelfth Night.

Well-rotted manure: manure which is full of worms, smells sweet and in which the constituent parts are indistinguishable.

Whip: one-year old fruit tree comprising a single stem only.

Widger: small flattened tool used to carefully and gently lift seedlings out of their trays in advance of potting-up.

Windfall: apple, pear or plum which has fallen naturally from the tree and can be harvested by simply bending over and picking up.

Wind-rock: damage caused by the wind, especially low down at the crown.

Index

On The Plot

Visit our How To website at www.howto.co.uk

At **www.howto.co.uk** you can engage in conversation with our authors – all of whom have 'been there and done that' in their specialist fields. You can get access to special offers and additional content, but most importantly you will be able to engage with, and become a part of, a wide and growing community of people just like yourself.

At **www.howto.co.uk** you'll be able to talk and share tips with people who have similar interests and are facing similar challenges in their lives. People who, just like you, have the desire to change their lives for the better – be it through moving to a new country, starting a new business, growing their own vegetables, or writing a novel.

At **www.howto.co.uk** you'll find the support and encouragement you need to help make your aspirations a reality.

You can go direct to www.good-home-cooking.co.uk, which is part of the main How To site.

How To Books strives to present authentic, inspiring, practical information in its books. Now, when you buy a title from **How To Books,** you get even more than just words on a page.

GLOUCESTERSHIRE COUNTY COUNCIL	9933411C71	Bertrams	AN	
		06/10/2009	£12.99	

HASHMAN JOE
On the plot with 'Dirt
308619/00003 - 1 of 1

Also published by Spring Hill

A Vegetable Gardener's Year
by Dirty Nails

This book is for vegetable gardeners and nature-lovers everywhere. It is a grow your own manual, a recipe book, and a store of fascinating observations about natural history in the garden.

This is a book that can be taken to bed as an end-of-day muse, or get dog-eared and dirty as an essential aid to cultivating and cooking home-grown food.

Here's what they are saying about the author, *Blackmore Vale Magazine* columnist Dirty Nails:

"Plain common sense, humour, and an amazing eye for detail . . . really does tick all the boxes" *Grow It*

"Simple, down to earth style and chatty text . . . a delightful walk through the garden year." *Garden News*

If you have ever dreamed about growing and cooking your own food, living the good life and getting close to nature, then this is the book for you! Gardening and natural history enthusiast Joe Hashman (alias 'Dirty Nails' of the *Blackmore Vale Magazine*) serves up another absorbing helping of practical tips, advice, observations and recipes from his vegetable plot and kitchen.

In this week-by-week account of the fruit and vegetable gardener's year, you are invited to join Joe on the plot and get stuck in to the important jobs of the day.

The finer points of crop husbandry are beautifully and clearly presented using simple step-by-step colour photographs. With poetic licence in his writing, the author takes readers on a wonderful journey of discovery through the changing seasons. A wealth of easy to follow but unusual recipes will keep the chef in you busy and satisfied too!

Joe's first book, **How to Grow Your Own Food,** was published by Spring Hill in 2007 and received widespread critical acclaim. His down-to-earth style and quirky tales from the garden continued with the release of *A Vegetable Gardener's Year* (2008). This latest volume stands alone as a manual for both the first time grower or seasoned expert, and perfectly complements his earlier titles in the ongoing quest for success and satisfaction on the plot.

Writing as 'Dirty Nails', Joe's popular weekly columns have been enjoyed by the readers of the Dorset-based *Blackmore Vale Magazine* since 2004. He now contributes to newspapers across England and Wales on a regular basis.

Cover design: www.mousematdesign.com
Front cover photograph: The Garden Picture Library

£12.99

ISBN 978-1-905862-32-0

9 781905 862320

info@howtobooks.co.uk
www.howtobooks.co.uk

Gardening/Cookery